Alex La Guma

Twayne's World Authors Series
African Literature

Bernth Lindfors, Editor
The University of Texas at Austin

TWAS 743

ALEX LA GUMA
(1925-   )
Photograph courtesy of Alex La Guma

Alex La Guma

By Cecil A. Abrahams

Bishop's University

Twayne Publishers • Boston

Alex La Guma

Cecil A. Abrahams

Copyright © 1985 by G.K. Hall & Company
All Rights Reserved
Published by Twayne Publishers
A Division of G.K. Hall & Company
70 Lincoln Street
Boston, Massachusetts 02111

Printed on permanent/durable acid-free
paper and bound in the United States of
America

Library of Congress Cataloging in Publication Data

Abrahams, Cecil Anthony.
  Alex La Guma.

   (Twayne's world authors series ; TWAS 743. African
literature)
   Bibliography: p.
   Includes index.
   1. La Guma, Alex — Criticism and interpretation.
I. Title.   II. Series: Twayne's world authors series ;
TWAS 743.   III. Series: Twayne's world authors series.
African literature.
PR9369.3.L3Z58   1985   823   84-15653
ISBN 0-8057-6589-1

Contents

About the Author

Cecil A. Abrahams received the Ph.D. from the University of Alberta for a study of the work of the English romantic poet William Blake. Born in South Africa and educated in South Africa and Canada, he is currently Professor of English literature at Bishop's University in Canada. He has published the book William Blake's Fourfold Man and his numerous essays and reviews on African, Caribbean, Canadian, and British literature have appeared in many journals and books.

Preface

In the essay "Culture and Liberation," Alex La Guma argues that "life is the stimulation of artistic endeavour," and since life embraces "man's struggle to reach higher levels of civilization," art must perforce address the central questions that involve life• (1). Born into a home where his father was an active member of the Communist party of South Africa and a militant union organizer, and nurtured in a stultifying social environment of poverty and oppression, La Guma from his early twenties has kept before his mind the need for art and life to be inseparable. For him, art acts as a subversive force against restriction and it provides for man an opportunity to envision an existence that transcends the ugly reality of oppression. In keeping with his heartfelt belief that art is related to sociopolitical life, he has succeeded in both the mundane and imaginative worlds to follow a path that has furthered his vision.

La Guma entered the worlds of journalism and creative writing after he had already served an important apprenticeship as a political activist. Throughout his long career as a short-story writer, a novelist, and once more a journalist, he has continued his active political life on behalf of the liberation struggle inside and outside South Africa. His career in journalism gave him a necessary outlet to describe the plight of the Cape colored community, and when he inevitably took up his pen to write short stories he naturally chose to write about the people with whom he lived and suffered. La Guma recognized the almost total absence of treatment of his community in South African literature and consciously sat down to be the social historian of the Cape colored people. Out of this endeavor came his first two novels, A Walk in the Night and And a Threefold Cord. Both of these books deal with well-known colored districts of Cape Town and with people and problems that are familiar to these areas. Here already La Guma hoped that by pointing out to his community the many aspects of unjust

treatment that exist in South Africa the colored community would become infuriated enough to marshal forces
behind the antiracist struggle.

While the first two novels were conceived and exe-
cuted, La Guma spent several terms in detention for his
defiant actions of protest against the South African
government. Out of these experiences he was able to
write his third novel, The Stone Country. The book
deals with prison life and the oppressive conditions that
prevail there. It also follows logically the movement of
those colored South Africans who in frustration at the
lives they live in the first two novels violate the
unjust laws and end up in prison. The last two novels,
In the Fog of the Season's End and Time of the Butcherbird, were created once La Guma had left South Africa to
live in exile in the United Kingdom. In these novels he
shifts from being the social historian of the colored
community and concentrates instead on the resistance
struggle in South Africa. Whereas in In the Fog of the
Season's End the writer is chiefly concerned with the
establishment and the processes of the struggle, in Time
of the Butcherbird the resisters have finally come into
contact with their oppressors and begin to score vic-
tories over them.

La Guma's work cuts to the heart of the central issues
in South Africa. He has created works of art that are
memorable and that address the serious questions of
racism and freedom in South Africa. He has attempted to
show his fellow oppressed that the unjust laws that bind
him and his people are devised to obstruct them from
developing their full potential to destroy those laws.
Finding such a truthful and defiant vision unpalatable,
the South African regime has gone to great lengths to
stifle and destroy his work and person. But even though
his work and words are banned in his native land, his
fiery message of a better and hopeful South Africa rages
on both outside the country and in clandestine gatherings
inside the country.

The purpose of this study is to explore and to develop
the many aspects of La Guma's vision of a liberated South
Africa. The first chapter provides biographical details
of an active political and creative life. The second
chapter studies in some depth the fourteen short stories
that La Guma wrote. Chapter 3 provides a close, analyti-
cal reading of A Walk in the Night. Chapter 4 studies
And a Threefold Cord. Chapters 5, 6, and 7 provide,

respectively, close readings of The Stone Country, In the Fog of the Season's End, and Time of the Butcher-bird.

I am grateful to Alex La Guma for allowing me generous time and unstinted help and for permission to quote from his published and unpublished work. It is through the many long conversations with him in London and Havana that I was able to form an intimate idea of his work. I owe a large debt to Blanche La Guma as well. She often supplied missing details of her husband's life and contributed greatly to the delightful hospitality and humorous moments we shared. I would also like to thank Steve and Sheila Tobias, who extended to me their hospitality while I was doing research in London. And for financial and academic assistance I wish to express my gratitude to Bishop's University and the Social Sciences and Humanities Research Council of Canada.

Cecil A. Abrahams

Bishop's University

Chronology

19th century	Lena Fruzela, maternal grandmother of Alex La Guma, arrives in Cape Town from Indonesia. Marries Scottish immigrant, Mr. Alexander, and gives birth to Wilhelmina Alexander, mother-to-be of Alex La Guma. Mr. La Guma, paternal grandfather, arrives in Cape Town from Malagasy. Son, James La Guma, father-to-be of Alex La Guma, is born in 1894.
1924	James La Guma and Wilhelmina Alexander marry.
1925	February 20, Alex La Guma born in District Six, Cape Town.
1932	Enters Upper Ashley Primary School, Cape Town.
1933	Only sister, Joan, born.
1938	Enters Trafalgar High School, Cape Town. Volunteers to join International Brigade against fascism in Spain. Offer refused.
1940	Offers to serve in World War II. Offer refused because of physical build and age.
1942	Leaves high school without graduating.
1942-1943	Employed in a warehouse making parcels and moving furniture.
1944	Employed by Metal Box Company, Cape Town, as factory worker.
1945	Completes matriculation examinations as a night student at the Cape Technical College.
1946	Joins strike executive committee at Metal Box Company and organizes strike for better work-

ing conditions and wages. Dismissed from job. Becomes politically active.

1947-1954 Works as bookkeeper for a few traders. Works as a clerk in an American petroleum company, Cape Town.

1947 Joins Young Communist League and becomes active speaker at meetings.

1948 Afrikaner Nasionale party wins election on platform of apartheid. Becomes member of the Communist party of South Africa, District 20.

1950 Communist party declared illegal organization by the state. Listed as a known Communist under the Suppression of Communism Act.

1954 Marries Blanche Herman, a nurse and midwife. Member of Executive Committee of the South African Coloured Peoples Organization (SACPO). Later known as the Coloured Peoples Congress (CPC).

1955 Elected chairman of SACPO and organizes Cape delegation to the Congress of the People in Johannesburg in June 1955. Detained by police at Beaufort West, Cape Province, while on the way to Congress of the People. Employed by New Age as a reporter.

1956 Gives leadership in Cape Town bus boycott. Son Eugene born. Arrested with 155 other anti-racist leaders and charged with high treason against the state.

1957 Assigned "Up My Alley" column in New Age. Elected to National Executive of Coloured Peoples Congress. First short story, "Etude" (later known as "Nocturne"), published in New Age.

1958 Attempt made on his life.

1959 Second son, Bartholomew, born.

1960   Treason trial ends with acquittal of all the
        accused. Sharpeville Massacre. Assassination
        attempt on Prime Minister Verwoerd and declara-
        tion of state of emergency. Detained for
        seven months at Roeland Street jail and
        Worcester prison under state of emergency.

1961   Detained for ten days for organizing general
        strike. Father, James La Guma, dies of heart
        ailment at age sixty-seven.

1962   Publication of A Walk in the Night. Banned
        under Suppression of Communism Act. Forced to
        resign job with New Age and not permitted to
        participate in political activities.

1963   Detained for five months in Roeland Street
        jail on suspicion of aiding underground move-
        ment of the African National Congress.
        Blanche La Guma also arrested but released.
        Placed under five-year house arrest. Unable
        to leave home or communicate with friends or
        family. Wife and children given special
        permission to live with him. Death of La
        Guma's mother.

1964   Publication of And a Threefold Cord.

1966   Detained for four months in Maitland and
        Roeland Street police stations for sus-
        picion of promoting work of the banned
        Communist party of South Africa. Leaves
        South Africa with family for London on an
        exit permit.

1966-1967   Travels extensively throughout the United
            Kingdom to speak on the situation in South
            Africa. Tour arranged by International Anti-
            Apartheid Movement.

1966-1968   Employed by a private radio agency owned by
            Dennis Duerden. Tasks include reviewing of
            books, discussion of work of other writers,
            commentaries, scripts for short plays, and
            writing of the Captain Zondie detective
            stories.

1967   Publication of The Stone Country. Attends Scandinavian-African Writers Conference in Stockholm. Attends Fourth Congress of the Union of Soviet Writers Association in Moscow. Attends Third Congress of the Afro-Asian Writers Association in Beirut.

1968-1970   Employed as an insurance clerk for Abbey Insurance Company in London.

1969   Awarded the Lotus Prize by the Afro-Asian Writers Association for his creative work.

1970   Invited to accept award at the Fourth Congress of the Afro-Asian Writers Association in New Delhi, India. Indira Gandhi presents prizes to La Guma and Agostinho Neto.

1970-1978   Serves as chairman of the London district of the African National Congress.

1971   Edits book, Apartheid.

1972   Publication of In the Fog of the Season's End.

1975   Attends Fifth Congress of the Afro-Asian Writers Association in Tashkent, USSR. Elected deputy secretary-general of the association. Tours Soviet Union for six weeks. Visits Chile as a delegate to the World Peace Congress. Visits Vietnam as a delegate to the World Peace Congress.

1976   Writer-in-residence at the University of Dar es Salaam, Tanzania.

1977   Becomes acting secretary-general of the Afro-Asian Writers Association.

1978   Publication of A Soviet Journey. Appointed chief representative of the African National Congress in the Caribbean with residence in Havana, Cuba.

1979   Publication of Time of the Butcherbird.

Elected secretary-general of the Afro-Asian Writers Association.

1982-1985   Writing "Zone of Fire." Continues work as chief representative of the African National Congress in the Caribbean.

Chapter One
Politics and Art:
The Creative Activist

At the beginning of the nineteenth century the British
took over the control and administration of the Cape of
Good Hope from Holland. The significant Dutch-settler
community at the Cape resented this takeover and the use
of the English language. Since there was a raging debate
in the British Parliament concerning the treatment of
slaves in British colonies, the large indigenous slave
population that the Dutch settlers had acquired by force
came under severe scrutiny from the British administration at the Cape. Hence, when the British Parliament
decided to emancipate all slaves in their colonies, the
settler community at the Cape saw it as an unpalatable
affront to their survival as a people. A large part of
the community decided in 1833 to trek inland. Here the
settler community, now known as Boers (literally,
"farmers"), came into contact with a variety of black
groups. Since the settlers were in search of territory
to raise livestock and the indigenous population was
engaged in the same activity, wars between the Boers and
the blacks often occurred. Through superior weaponry the
Boers were able to establish their hegemony as far as the
provinces of the Orange Free State and the Transvaal by
the third quarter of the nineteenth century.

Meanwhile, at the Cape, the settlers who remained
imported nonwhite immigrants from the former Dutch
colonies. Since these were chiefly urban settlers, many
of their servants were brought to the Cape to serve as
cooks, waitresses, gardeners, nannies, and house-cleaning
servants. It is "during the course of the nineteenth
century" (1) that Alex La Guma's family tree was planted
in South Africa. His grandmother on his mother's side, a
Miss Lena Fruzela, came from Indonesia but she was of
Dutch and Indonesian origins and was brought to South
Africa to work as a cook. Later she was employed at the
Parliament building as a cook and waitress. While being
employed there she was approached by a Mr. John X.

Merriman, a Member of Parliament, to be his mistress.
She declined this offer. Noting this fact, La Guma with
a glint in the eye observes: "I suppose it might have al-
tered the course of history if she'd accepted" (2). Lena
Fruzela did, however, go on to marry a Scottish immigrant
carpenter by the name of Alexander, a name that was to be
passed on to La Guma at birth in the twentieth century.
From this marriage resulted the birth of Wilhelmina
Alexander, the mother-to-be of Alex La Guma. This marriage of Lena Fruzela to a white immigrant was not uncom-
mon in the nineteenth or earlier centuries. From the
time that the Dutch settlers and administrators landed at
the Cape there was cohabitation among the white and black
groups. The result of this was the origin of the Cape
colored population, which has now grown to over three
million people.

The grandparents of La Guma on his father's side
arrived at the Cape in the nineteenth century. They
originated from Malagasy but were of Indonesian and
German extraction. La Guma observes that he was told by
"an expert on the East Indies" that "the reason why we
have La in front of our name is that in the particular
part of the East Indian islands that my father's family
hailed from all the families have La in front of their
names" (3). James La Guma, the father-to-be of Alex, was
born in 1894. He was apprenticed in Cape Town as a
leather worker and as a shoe and harness maker. After
his apprenticeship he worked "at various odd jobs until
he ran away from home and went to South-West Africa to
work for the German colonialists on the farms, in the
harbor of Luberitz and in the diamond fields" (4). While
working in South-West Africa, James La Guma organized a
branch of the Industrial and Commercial Workers Union
(ICU) and led the workers in a strike at Pomona. In 1919
he was summoned to the headquarters of the ICU in Cape
Town and offered a position under the head of the union,
Mr. Clements Kadalie. Later he was promoted to the position of administrative secretary. In 1933 he helped to
organize the garment workers of the Cape Province and was
arrested.

The Communist party of South Africa, consisting at the
time of a small band of mainly white, English-speaking
South Africans, was the only political party at the time
that cared for the plight of the black workers. It was
inevitable, therefore, that James La Guma's committed
interests should coincide with those of the Communist

party. In 1924 he became a member, and when the party was banned in 1950 he was a member of the Central Committee.

In 1924 James La Guma married Wilhelmina Alexander, and on February 20, 1925, Alex La Guma was born in District Six, Cape Town. Eight years later, the only other child in the family, his sister Joan, was born. Wilhelmina La Guma worked in a cigarette factory to help keep the family "from dying of starvation" (5). But at night she returned to her young children to tend to them as well as to manage her household. According to La Guma, she was a kind and generous mother and a devoted wife and "carried on all the ordinary chores of a hard life like the rest of the women in District Six" (6). His father, on the other hand, was kept busy with his union and political work, and the young Alex remembers the staging of many political meetings at his home (7). The La Guma home was often filled with progressive political discussion, and although the children were not indoctrinated, the political attitudes of the father and friends rubbed off on the children (8).

Although busy in public work, James La Guma cared much for his children's education and was, as La Guma remembers, "one of my chief backers" (9). It is he who introduced Alex to the great works of literature and politics and ensured that there was always a steady supply of reading material for his children. It was he as well who encouraged La Guma's writing talents. This is how La Guma sees his father's influence on his life:

> My father had a great deal to do with molding my philosophical and political outlook and guiding me towards the reading of serious works, both political and literary. He himself was an avid reader, and I suppose this had something to do with my development one way or the other. My father died in 1961; that was just before my first novel came out, A Walk in the Night. I suppose one could say that he didn't see the fruits of his encouragement. (10)

The young Alex entered Upper Ashley Primary School in 1932. The school was situated "up on the hill above Cape Town" (11). The principal of the school was a Mrs. Petersen, whom he remembers as "a very strict, severe, and nevertheless kind woman who intended to make sure that we would grow up into decent and honest citizens" (12). As

was natural most of his friends came from the area
surrounding his school.   La Guma remembers his school
days as adventurous times and that he had numerous
friends (13).   But one friend in particular, a boy named
Daniel, stands out in his memory:

> I remember a particular boyfriend of mine, Daniel, who
> lived just opposite to my house.   He was of African
> color, but in those days there was no sort of formal
> segregation or apartheid.   People in the working-class
> areas lived mixed up, Africans, coloreds, Indians.
> Anyway, Daniel was an African boy of my own age and we
> were great chums and he was a great favorite of mine
> because he was a cheerful, lighthearted fellow and we
> spent a lot of time as children together.   But then
> with the development of residential segregation Daniel
> and his family had to move out.   His parents moved to
> Langa, which is just outside of Cape Town.   And it was
> the last I saw of Daniel for many, many years.   Then
> suddenly one day when I was grown up, working, earning
> a living, I met Daniel again.   He was not the same
> Daniel I had known before.   He had become a gangster,
> been to prison, and his whole life before him didn't
> hold any sort of rosy prospects.   It was quite a
> moving, touching experience for me to meet again an
> old school friend who had become a victim of the
> circumstances which he couldn't cope with.   (14)

It is the Daniel of La Guma's early years who becomes
"one of the models" for the character Michael Adonis in
A Walk in the Night (15).
      The segregation of races in residential areas is one
of the earliest experiences that the writer had with the
racist system.   But his very first, powerful experience
came when his mother took him to the circus.   This is how
La Guma describes this event:

> I was very young, about seven or eight years old, when
> my mother took me to the circus for the first time.
> Anyway, the circus was on, and for children it was
> very exciting.   When we were in the big top watching
> the performance I discovered that I couldn't see any-
> thing that was going on in the ring.   For some reason
> or another the performers were always looking the
> other way, performing in the other direction.   I asked
> my mother why this was so and she told me we were

sitting in the seats for black people and the main
concentration of the circus was on the white audience,
so we just had to take our chance with the entertain-
ment being provided. That was the first and last time
that I ever went to a circus in South Africa. The
next time I attended a circus was in Europe as an
exile, and at that time I reflected back with a certain amount of sadness over that first situation, my
first experience with racial discrimination. (16)

This incident appears later in In the Fog of the Season's End when Beukes remembers being taken by his aunt
"to a circus once when I was a lighty" (17). A second
incident the writer remembers is also detailed in In the
Fog of the Season's End. On this occasion he was among
many students who had been invited to sing at a white
school. He was quite surprised to know that there were
schools for different race groups [Fog, pp. 83-84].
    In 1938 La Guma entered Trafalgar High School in Cape
Town. His academic record was not "very good," not
because "I was dumb or stupid" but rather because his
interests were outside the schoolroom and in Europe,
where the battle against Spanish, German, and Italian
fascism was taking place (18). As he says,

the world was then confronted with the Fascist uprisings in Europe and naturally, being a member of a
political family, one got the news of these events all
the time. The events were discussed in the family and
at the meetings which took place in our house. This
encouraged the somewhat romantic side of my character.
(19)

The consequence was that at the age of thirteen La Guma
volunteered to serve in the International brigade in the
civil war in Spain between the forces of democracy and
fascism. This "boyish dream" led him to learn "a few
words of Spanish" (20). Needless to say, his youthful
offer was refused.
    Although he did not care much for in-class education,
La Guma "loved reading books" and received much of his
education through this source:

I loved reading books. Since early childhood I was
always looking for books. I read at first the books
that children loved: Robert Louis Stevenson, Dumas,

Victor Hugo, and so on. Then I read adventure stories, westerns, detective stories, and gradually
began to turn towards the more serious classics such
as Shakespeare, the Russian authors, Tolstoy, Gorky,
and then the American writers, James T. Farrell,
Steinbeck, and Hemingway. Whenever I could lay my
hands on a book I took the opportunity. In fact, I
used to use my meager pocket money to buy books at
secondhand bookstores and sometimes I had saved enough
to enjoy the luxury of buying a book at an expensive
bookstore. (21)

When La Guma was fifteen years old and still at high
school, the world went to war against Fascist Germany.
His father had been accepted by the army and he served
in the Cape Corps in Abyssinia and Egypt. The young La
Guma offered his services as well, but, as he observes,
"I was fifteen years old and very skinny and the recruit-
ing sergeant just gave me one look and told me to clear
off" (22). His interest in the war, however, did not
abate and when he reached his matriculation year in 1942
he decided to leave school. He completed high school at
the Cape Technical College later while he was employed as
a "worker." His first job was in a warehouse, where he
"made parcels and moved furniture" (23). But then he
decided in a "romantic" way that he would like to work in
a factory because it would put him "closer to the ordinary working people" (24). He obtained a position at the
Metal Box Company in Cape Town, where he worked "for
about two years manufacturing tin cans and such-like
products" (25). He lost his job at the factory because
he was a member of the strike committee, which organized
a strike for better wages and working conditions. La
Guma worked as a bookkeeper for a few traders and later
for an oil company in Cape Town and, finally, as a
reporter.

It was not until La Guma was employed at the Metal Box
Company that he showed any real interest in becoming
actively involved with the antiracist struggle of the
day. He now found himself attending meetings and demon-
strations and participating in various pickets related to
the workers' struggle. Then in 1948 the Afrikaner
Nasionale party was elected to govern South Africa and
their policies of apartheid brought a new wave of agita-
tion against racism and oppression. The year before the
victory of the Nasionale party La Guma joined the young

Communist League and became an "active speaker at meetings" (26). In 1948 he was transferred to the Communist
party of South Africa and became a member of District 20.
In 1950 the South African government banned the Communist party and La Guma was listed under the Suppression
of Communism Act as a known Communist.

In 1954 La Guma married Blanche Herman, a nurse and
midwife, after a short courtship. They had known each
other at high school, but for a long period of time they
had not seen each other. Blanche had gone on to study
nursing and midwifery at the very well known St. Monica's
maternity home in Cape Town. Since her work was among
the poor of Cape Town, she developed a strong sense of
justice and worked actively in the political movement for
the betterment of conditions for the poor. It was while
she was engaged in political work that she saw Alex La
Guma again and reestablished her relationship with him.
Blanche recalls that "Alex was always a romantic,"
because on their "very first date he proposed marriage"
(27). Although Blanche accepted the proposal, she knew
that she would still have to convince her father that a
listed Communist and barely employable person such as La
Guma "would be able to take care of her" (28). Mr.
Herman accepted Blanche's choice but was adamant that the
marriage be blessed in a church ceremony. On this occasion La Guma laid aside his nonreligious belief and
permitted the marriage to take place in a church (29).
One of La Guma's fondest portraits of his father-in-law
is that of Frances's father listening to a rugby match in
In the Fog of the Season's End [Fog, p. 93]. The
Frances of this novel, however, is not Blanche but "one
of the girls I courted before I met Blanche" (30).

In 1954 La Guma became a member of the Executive
Committee of the newly founded South African Coloured
Peoples Organization (SACPO). In 1955 he became chairman
of the organization. In this year he was chosen as one
of the organizers of SACPO for the Congress of the
People, which was held in Kliptown, Johannesburg, in June
1955. The Congress was convened to solidify the work of
all antiracist groups and to unify them under the banner
of the African National Congress of South Africa. A
large Cape province contingent was led by Alex La Guma,
but the participants were stopped at Beaufort West in the
Cape by the police and instead of attending the Congress
they spent the weekend "sleeping on their lorries" (31).
This frustrating act on the part of the racist authority

did not dampen the determination of the oppressed because
they returned to the Cape even more prepared to carry on
the struggle. La Guma expressed the feelings of the people as follows: "The task ahead of the South African
Coloured Peoples Organization and the other sponsoring
organizations is to carry the Freedom Charter to every
corner of the land and to acquaint all those who are outside the liberatory struggle with the ideas embodied in
it" (32). And later in the same paper La Guma indicated
that "what started as a big disappointment turned into a
most happy and productive week-end" because they were
able to form Congress branches, sing freedom songs and inform the residents of Beaufort West of the struggle (33).

The Congress of the People frightened the governing
party and the security police now stepped up their
arrests while many leaders of the movement were banned.
In responding to this new wave of attacks, La Guma empha-
sized "that police raids, bannings and imprisonment would
not stop the struggle—that the movement was bigger than
the leaders" (34). As chairman of SACPO, now known as
the Coloured Peoples Congress (CPC), La Guma's public
speeches and protest activities came under careful scrutiny by the police. He gave leadership in attacking the
government's 1955 Race Classification Bill and the 1956
South African Act Amendment Bill, which removed colored
voters from the common electoral roll. He protested the
Cape Town City Council's decision in 1956 to segregate
the beaches and he led the bus boycott of April and May
1956 when the Cape Town municipal authority decided to
segregate the buses. On that occasion he stated that
"the people of Cape Town have shown they are prepared to
fight back against the government's racialist madness,"
and he saw this campaign as "part of the struggle against
Apartheid as a whole" (35). And in a May Day message the
following defiant statement was made:

To all the workers and oppressed people of South
Africa I extend, on this great day, my sincere greet-
ings and good wishes for a democratic, happy and peaceful future. May Day this year is defiled with
increasing oppression by the ruling class and the
Nationalist tyrants. Police terrorism and violence is
rife. "White baasskap" and "Christian civilization"
marches to the crack of the sjambok, the hose-pipe and
the stengun. But on the other hand May Day is greeted
and raised to glorious heights by the heroic struggles

of the oppressed people against Apartheid, pass laws, removals, deportations and economic exploitation— for the new life of the Freedom Charter. Day by day the unity of the oppressed peoples of the world grows stronger. From Africa to Asia the forces of anti-imperialism, peace and friendship are marching forward. The sun of colonial slavery and war is setting fast. Down with Apartheid! Forward to the Freedom Charter! Down with Imperialism and War! Long live New Democracy, Peace and International Solidarity. (36)

On December 13, 1956, he and 155 antiracist leaders throughout South Africa were arrested and charged with treason against the state.

The treason trial was held in Johannesburg and literally dragged on from 1956 to early 1960, when the presiding judge dismissed all the allegations of the state against the accused. During this lengthy period La Guma was not permitted to participate in political activities. His only public function was that of being a columnist for New Age, where he received a reduced salary. Since this was also the year that his first son, Eugene, who now is married and lives in the Soviet Union, was born, the financial responsibility for the family depended very much on Blanche La Guma.

La Guma began his career in journalism in 1955 with the progressive, left-wing weekly New Age. Before 1955 he had done "a couple of pieces for the old Guardian" (37). The Guardian was banned by the South African regime in 1954 because it tended to be a progressive, liberal-minded newspaper that refused to follow the official government policy on race relations. This paper was succeeded for a short time by Advance, which was also banned for the same reasons as those given for the Guardian's discontinuance. New Age first appeared on October 28, 1954, and its editor and one of the owners, R. K. Cope, promised that the newspaper would continue to follow the tradition of the Guardian and Advance in opposing the excesses of the Afrikaner regime and of supporting the legitimate aspirations of the black community in the spirit of

freedom for all men and women in South Africa. Freedom of conscience, of the Press and speech and of assembly and movement. Democracy and the restoration

of the rule of law in South Africa. Peace between all
races and between nation and nation. Equal political,
social and cultural rights for all and the removal of
discrimination on grounds of colour, race or beliefs.
(38)

The owners of New Age were liberal-minded, white,
English-speaking South Africans who recognized that their
paper tended to appeal to a clientele with similar cultural and intellectual background as themselves. To
succeed in carrying out the objectives that they had
established in their first edition and to increase their
readership among the nonwhite community, the owners of
the newspaper sought staff within the black community.
Since La Guma was an active participant in the shaping of
the Cape colored community, and because he had demonstrated in the Guardian his competence as a writer, he
was chosen for one of the positions at New Age.
    Most of La Guma's reports in New Age deal with the
conditions of life of the Cape colored community. For
example, in a piece called "A Pick and Shovel," he
describes the dismal position of the colored people in
South Africa. He observes that they live "in the slums"
where people "huddle, sleep on staircases and in packed
rooms" (39). "Everywhere," he notes,

is the smell of stale cooking, sweat and stagnant
water. On the corners groups gather in the lamplight
and the dice come out and the pennies and tickies
[three pennies] clink on the asphalt. Somewhere a
guitar twangs quietly and then ripples as skillful,
self-taught fingers fly along the frets. When the
pubs close the shebeens are open for business . . .
the cheapest wine costs three-and-sixpence a bottle,
and brandy ranges from fifteen to twenty-five shillings. It is whispered that the big houses pay protection to keep the police away. The census declares
that we are almost one-and-a-quarter million. But if
you identify a people, not by names and the colour of
their skin, but by hardship and joy, pleasure and
suffering, cherished hopes and broken dreams, the
grinding monotony of toil without gain, despair and
starvation, illiteracy, tuberculosis and malnutrition,
laughter and vice, ignorance, genius, superstition,
ageless wisdom and undying confidence, love and
hatred, then you will have to give up counting. (40)

Several of his articles deal with the lives of the
"skollies" or gangsters of District Six. In an article
of September 20, 1956, he gives the reader a vivid
description of both "The Dead-End Kids of Hanover Street"
and District Six. This portrait of Cape Town street life
reappears later in A Walk in the Night:

> From Castle Bridge to Sheppard Street, Hanover Street
> runs through the heart of District Six, and along it
> one can feel the pulse-beats of society. It is the
> main artery of the local world of haves and have-nots,
> the struggling and the idle, the weak and the strong.
> Its colour is in the bright enamel signs, the neon-
> lights, the shop-fronts, the littered gutters and
> draped washing. Pepsi-Cola. Commando Cigarettes.
> Sale Now On. Its life blood is the hawkers bawling
> their wares above the blare of jazz from the music
> shops. "Aaatappels [potatoes], ja. Uiwe [onions],
> ja," ragged youngsters leaping on and off the speeding
> trackless-trams with the agility of monkeys; harassed
> mothers getting in the groceries; shop assistants; The
> Durango Kids of 1956; and the knots of loungers under
> the balconies and in the rows of shops and cafe. . . .
> Most of these [Durango Kids] boys have had little
> or no education. From childhood they must augment the
> family income as newsboys and hawkers. The whole of
> life becomes a struggle to survive by any means whatso-
> ever. But they are nevertheless aware of some of the
> causes of their plight. . . . Hanging around and
> waiting. Slums, disease, unemployment, lack of educa-
> tion, the terrible weight of the colour-bar which with-
> holds the finer things of life—all help to grind them
> down until many of them become beasts of prey roaming
> an unfriendly jungle. (41)

Some of his other articles deal with the Roeland Street
jail (a jail with which he later was to become familiar
as an inmate) (42), his visits as a reporter to the law
courts (43), and his frequent attacks on the Cape Town
City Council for its failure to provide the colored population with proper housing, sewage, and transportation.
When the treason trial began in Johannesburg in
December 1956, La Guma's contributions to New Age
became less frequent, but when he returned periodically
to Cape Town he brought with him vivid descriptions of
the people and their morale at the trial and on the

outside. In an article called "They All Have Their
Troubles, but Nobody Complains," La Guma gives a good
description of the confident courage of the treason
trialists:

> I tried to find complaints, regrets, tearfulness among
> the accused, but instead there is only confidence,
> geniality and high spirits, all combined with in-
> destructible determination. Here is the spirit of
> man, the will to go forward, the courage to look ahead
> and submerge personal hardships for the common good.
> Here is the bricks and the mortar, the muscles and the
> sinews, the life blood that go into the building of a
> new life. (45)

On May 2, 1957, La Guma was assigned a regular column by
New Age. The column was called "Up My Alley" and he
continued to write it until he was prevented from doing
so by the government in June 1962. New Age itself was
banned in the fall of 1962. It was through the ironical,
humorous, and at times bitingly satirical column of "Up
My Alley" that La Guma became well known in Cape Town. A
random selection of the "Up My Alley" columns shows us
many of the concerns as well as the style of reporting
that have made La Guma's creative work familiar. In a
column on May 23, 1957, he argues characteristically that
"a society based on suppression, violence, armed force,
poverty and unemployment creates violence, bloodshed,
gangsterism and murder" (46). A story on September 26,
1957, deals with the eviction of a colored father from a
café into which his boy had wandered and been served a
soft drink because the owner of the café assumed that
the boy was white (47). In another column he discusses
the issue of overcrowding in colored community coaches on
the trains and wonders aloud when the smoldering resentment will lead to "the stage when everybody is going to
stay off the entire Apartheid system" (48).

Although La Guma was not permitted to participate in
political work during the time of the treason trial, he
was, as a sign of solidarity, elected to the National
Executive of the Coloured Peoples Congress in April 1957.
His father, James La Guma, was elected chairman. La
Guma did, however, continue to do political work behind
the scenes and he was considered enough of a threat by
the regime that an attempt was made on his life. On May
15, 1958, New Age reports that "two shots were fired by

an unknown person at Mr. Alex La Guma while he was
working in his study at his residence in Athlone" (49).
Three days after this unsuccessful attempt, he "received
an anonymous letter through the post reading 'Sorry we
missed you. Will call again. The Patriots'" (50).

Many of South Africa's black writers had their published creative beginnings in the field of journalism,
and it was no different with La Guma. According to him,
"when New Age asked me to take a job, that is when I
really started to write seriously. I suppose, inevitably, I sat down and wrote short stories" (51). But La
Guma's interest in writing goes back to his schooldays.
He observes that

> as a schoolboy I always put my pen to paper. On a
> couple of occasions I produced essays in school which
> were read out to the class. It didn't strike me as
> being the genius of authorship, but the teachers said
> that I had a certain talent for writing. I used to
> concoct stories which were, well, the kind a schoolboy
> would write—schoolboy adventures, and filling exer-
> cise books which mounted up at home. And I remember
> in the springtime when my mother cleaned out the
> house, then all my valuable manuscripts went into the
> garbage. (52)

La Guma notes further that he was popular among his
school friends because he had the ability "to spin yarns
almost at will and to command their attention" (53).

In 1957 his first short story, "Etude" (later known as
"Nocturne"), was published in New Age. As will be
shown in the next chapter, this story, which deals with a
robber and his love for music, already typifies many of
the characteristic autobiographical elements of La Guma's
writing. The writer's ability to view affectionately and
describe his character and his excellent reporting skills
come out very well. The fact that the first story was
published and received with praise encouraged La Guma to
write "Out of Darkness" soon afterwards. These stories
were followed by "A Glass of Wine," Slipper Satin," "A
Matter of Taste," and then he attempted the long story A
Walk in the Night. In this book, as will be shown
later, La Guma sets out consciously to write about the
difficulties that the colored community must experience
under apartheid and how some of the members of the community respond to those difficulties. A Walk in the Night

was written in 1959 and completed by April 1960. During
this period the writer made several visits to Johannesburg to appear at the marathon treason trial and continued to do his "Up My Alley" column for New Age. The
year 1959 also brought an addition to the La Guma family.
A second son, Bartholomew, was born. He is currently
studying photography in East Germany.

The year 1960 was very important in the history of
South Africa. It began with the conclusion of the treason
trial and the acquittal of all 156 accused. On March 21,
1960, black South Africans in Sharpeville decided to burn
their hateful pass books outside a police station. What
started off as a defiant but peaceful demonstration was
soon transformed into a massacre when South African
policemen fired on the demonstrators. Sixty-nine people
were killed and several hundred were injured. Before the
dust had settled on this shocking event Prime Minister
Verwoerd, who is regarded as the architect of the
apartheid system, was shot at and admitted in critical
condition to a hospital. These events created unprece-
dented fear and panic in the regime and its supporters,
and a state of emergency was declared, which gave the
regime an excuse to rearrest all the acquitted treason
trialists and hundreds of other opponents of the racist
politics. La Guma was taken first to the Roeland Street
prison in Cape Town and then to a special prison in
Worcester in the Cape. He was held without trial for
seven months.

After his release from prison toward the end of 1960,
La Guma returned to his post at New Age, but he continued to be active in the liberation struggle. When
Nelson Mandela, the leader of the African National
Congress, in May 1961 called upon all justice-loving
South Africans to boycott the celebrations of the newly
declared Republic of South Africa, La Guma helped to
organize the colored people of Cape Town in a general
strike. For this action he was detained for ten days.
Soon after his release his father, James La Guma, who
had been his mentor in his political and creative
careers, died of a heart ailment at the age of sixty-
seven. His mother died in 1963. His father missed seeing by a few months the publication in Nigeria of La
Guma's first novel, A Walk in the Night, in 1962. In
this year he was banned under the Suppression of
Communism Act. This meant that he could not attend
public gatherings and he was forced to resign his posi-

tion as a reporter and columnist for New Age.

The banning orders of the racist regime did not deter
La Guma from carrying on political work behind the
scenes. Ironically, this enforcement gave him more time
to concentrate on his creative work. In the period 1960
to 1965 he wrote the short stories "At the Portagee's,"
"Blankets," "Coffee for the Road," "Tattoo Marks and
Nails," "The Gladiators," "A Matter of Honour," and "The
Lemon Orchard." Between 1962 and 1963 he concentrated on
the writing of his second long work, And a Threefold
Cord, a novel that describes the conditions of poverty
in the slums of Cape Town. A part of this work was
completed in Roeland Street prison, where in 1963 La Guma
was detained for five months on suspicion of helping the
underground movement of the African National Congress in
producing "a leaflet of protest" (54). His wife,
Blanche, was also arrested but released soon afterward.
Upon La Guma's release in December 1963, he was immediate-
ly served a five-year house arrest order. The purpose of
the order was to assign him to his house for twenty-four
hours a day. "This meant," says La Guma,

> that I could not go beyond the gate of my house with-
> out permission from the authorities. It meant I
> couldn't work at any gainful employment. I was not
> permitted visitors. I even had to apply for a permit
> to have my wife share our house with me. The only
> oversight of the authorities was that they did not
> prevent me from using my pen. They have since seen
> how dangerous this can be and now they won't permit
> any form of writing. (55)

In 1964 And a Threefold Cord was published in East
Berlin. La Guma used his enforced solitary confinement
to record his observations of life in a South African
prison. Hence, from 1964 to 1965 he drafted his third
long work, The Stone Country. In 1966 he was arrested
once again and detained for four months without trial at
the Cape Town jail of Maitland and Roeland Street. On
this occasion he was held on suspicion of promoting the
underground work of the banned Communist party of South
Africa. He was released from jail in July 1966 and in
September of the same year he and his family were permitted to leave South Africa for London on permanent exit
visas. Since the External Mission of the African National Congress was in its beginning stages, he was persuaded

to accept exile so as to work for the liberation struggle
from outside South Africa. La Guma describes his decision as follows:

> Well, it was more of a mixture of decision and require-
> ments of the sort of political struggle. It was felt
> that after having spent four years under house arrest
> and going into the fifth year with the prospect of
> another five years there was no point in remaining
> locked up in one's home indefinitely. One could be
> more constructive and freer outside. So we came to
> Europe to carry on what we were doing on another
> front. (56)

As a writer leaving the terrain where until then all his
imaginative creations had occurred, La Guma reveals an
element of realistic sadness in the following statement:

> Well, for my writing, exile has been both good and
> bad. I would prefer to sit in South Africa and write
> books there. But, of course, the government would not
> allow me to write books in South Africa. So as a
> writer I am glad that in Europe I am able to produce
> all the works I have up to now. And so from that
> point of view it is a positive aspect of being in
> exile. But on the other hand having left sort of
> under extraordinary circumstances rather than volun-
> tarily, and the fact that one is all the time thinking
> of what one can produce as a writer about South Afri-
> ca, one would prefer to be there. (57)

And as if in anticipation of critics who argue that
exiled writers such as La Guma are too far removed from
their subject to continue to be authentic, he responds:

> Up to now I have had no difficulty keeping in contact
> with my lived subject. I don't know what the future
> holds for me. However, I do not agree with those
> people who argue that a writer cannot write about a
> situation when he is not present on the scene. I
> believe that if a writer cannot write about one situa-
> tion he has to go and write about another situation.
> He is a writer first. He is a South African writer
> because of circumstances. But if he is a writer with
> imagination he can write about other scenes, project

the same ideas that he is trying to project on other
stages, so to speak. So I suppose if I become dried
up in terms of South Africa, if I want to continue
writing then I will write about Britain, about somewhere else. I wrote a short story about the war in
Vietnam. It was published in Vietnam and in other
anthologies. So it shows that if you have talent and
ability you can project yourself into other situations. (58)

Once on the outside, La Guma threw himself energetical-
ly behind the work of the international Anti-Apartheid
Movement and throughout the rest of 1966 and most of 1967
he was the keynote speaker at antiapartheid gatherings in
the United Kingdom. Economically, however, life was not
easy for the La Gumas. Blanche La Guma worked for long
hours in dismal conditions at London hospitals, while La
Guma obtained employment at a private radio agency owned
by Dennis Duerden. From 1966 to 1968 he helped prepare
radio programs for broadcast in Africa for Deutsche
Welle. He also did book reviews and commentaries and
wrote short plays for broadcasting. He developed his own
series of detective plays based on a fictitious African
detective named Captain Zondie. According to La Guma,
this innovation gave him much pleasure, and he "looked
forward to producing the next chapter of the intriguing
saga" (59). Unfortunately, the agency went out of business in 1968.

The year 1967 was a busy one for La Guma. His recent
arrival from South Africa provided him with celebrated
status and he was in demand in many circles. Furthermore, his reputation as a writer of commitment was
enhanced when The Stone Country appeared in London in
1967. Soon after this publication, he was invited to
participate in a Scandinavian-African writers conference
in Stockholm. Here he met for the first time many black
writers of Africa who had already emerged as major names
in African literature. He also took the opportunity to
discuss the role of the black writer in an oppressive
country such as South Africa. Soon after his Stockholm
visit, he left for Moscow to be a guest of the Union of
Soviet Writers at their Fourth Congress. This visit to
the Soviet Union was the first of many to come.

In 1967 the Afro-Asian Writers Association gathered in
Beirut for their Third Congress. Once more, La Guma was

invited as a guest and a major speaker; and, once again,
he established lasting relations with writers from Africa
and Asia. Although his work received recognition in many
countries, he found that he was still financially unable
to devote most of his attention to his ceative work.
When the private radio agency folded, he found work of a
congenial nature hard to come by. He finally accepted a
position as an insurance clerk at Abbey Insurance Company
in London. "It seemed," according to La Guma, "as if
every exiled South African was employed by this company"
(60). He worked for the firm from 1968 to 1970. The
work "was laborious and boring and made me feel very
depressed" (61). He was delighted, therefore, when in
1969 he was awarded the first Lotus Prize for Literature
by the Afro-Asian Writers Association. Hence, when he
was invited in 1970 to New Delhi to accept the award from
Prime Minister Indira Gandhi on the occasion of the
Fourth Congress of the Afro-Asian Writers Association, he
gladly resigned his insurance job. La Guma, the late
Angolan president Agostinho Neto, and the Vietnamese
writer To Hoai were honored at the same ceremony.

     After a short holiday in India with his wife, La Guma
returned to London and worked furiously on his fourth
book, In the Fog of the Season's End. While doing so,
he continued to be active in the liberation struggle,
serving from 1970 to 1978 as chairman of the London
district of the African National Congress. His tasks
included chairing of meetings, organizing political
events, giving keynote speeches, and traveling inside and
outside London to make people aware of the struggle. He
also edited in 1971 for Seven Seas Publishers in East
Berlin a book of writings on apartheid by several committed South Africans.

     In 1972 In the Fog of the Season's End appeared in
London. As will be shown later, this was the most autobiographical work to date. Much of the novel had been
drafted in South Africa but fully written in London. In
this book he deals with the liberation struggle and his
own involvement therein. The book received critical
acclaim and confirmed La Guma's status as a major
literary figure in African literature.

     The next eventful year in La Guma's creative and
political life was in 1975. He attended the Fifth
Congress of the Afro-Asian Writers Association at Tashkent in the Soviet Union. At this congress he was

elected deputy secretary general of the association.
Later in 1975 he was invited by the Writers Union of the
Soviet Union to undertake a six-week tour of the country
and to record his impressions in book form. La Guma had
visited the Soviet Union on several occasions before;
hence, he used his impressions of the earlier visits and
combined them with his new experiences and wrote A
Soviet Journey. This book was published in Moscow in
1978. In 1975 as well, as a delegate to the World Peace
Congress, he had the opportunity to visit Chile a few
months before the Chilean armed forces deposed and
assassinated President Allende. La Guma remembers the
Chile of Allende "as a place of inspiring confidence and
democratic behavior" and considers the president's death
"to have been a great tragedy for freedom and democracy"
(62). And again in 1975, as the "heroic struggle of the
Vietnamese people against the forces of aggression and
colonialism were coming to an end" (63), he visited Vietnam, also as a delegate to the World Peace Congress.
Again he was impressed by the "fortitude and perseverance
of the Vietnamese people and celebrated with them in
their moment of success" (64).

In January and February of 1976 he was invited to be
writer-in-residence at the University of Dar es Salaam in
Tanzania. Unfortunately for him, he suffered a heart
attack and was forced to return to London earlier than
expected. In 1977 he was appointed acting secretary-
general of the Afro-Asian Writers Association when the
Egyptian secretary-general of the association, Youssef
El-Sebai, was assassinated in Cyprus. During 1977 as
well La Guma was busy drafting his fourth long book,
Time of the Butcherbird. In 1978 the African National
Congress appointed him their chief representative in the
Caribbean with residence in Havana, Cuba. To date, La
Guma continues to occupy this position. In 1979, at the
Sixth Congress of the Afro-Asian Writers Association in
Luanda, he was appointed secretary-general of the associa-
tion. Also in 1979 Time of the Butcherbird was published in London. In this novel he continues to deal
with the liberation struggle and, in particular, with the
forced mass removal of blacks from their ancestral lands.
Currently La Guma is busy drafting his sixth long work,
tentatively called "Zone of Fire." In this work he recognizes that the struggle in South Africa is now on a war
footing, and he follows in fact the returned footsteps of

trained guerrilla fighters, Peter, Paul, and Michael,
whom the reader last saw in In the Fog of the Season's
End. Since the struggle for South Africa's liberation
continues to preoccupy La Guma's political and creative
life, it is fitting that he should continue to blend politics and art while in Cuba.

Chapter Two
The Tale Teller:
The Short Stories

In the previous chapter reference was made to the fact that Alex La Guma did not write "seriously" until he was offered a position by New Age in 1955. And, following in the footsteps of many other nonwhite South African journalists, he "inevitably . . . sat down and wrote short stories" (1). Before this appointment La Guma had written short pieces for Fighting Talk and the Guardian. In 1956 New Age organized a short-story competition and La Guma's submission, "Etude," was considered to be good enough to be published in the newspaper in January 1957. Encouraged by the reception of this story, he submitted his second story, "Out of Darkness," to the magazine Africa South. This story was published in October 1957. The first two stories were followed quickly by "A Glass of Wine" and "Slipper Satin," both of which appeared first in the journal Black Orpheus. Since then La Guma has published ten more stories, all but one dealing with life in South Africa. "At the Portagee's," "Tattoo Marks and Nails," and "Blankets" were first printed in Black Orpheus; "Coffee for the Road" in Modern African Stories; "A Matter of Taste," "The Gladiators," and "The Lemon Orchard" in the New African; "Late Edition" and "Thang's Bicycle" in Lotus. La Guma's stories have now been translated into fifteen languages and have appeared in a variety of book collections and journals.

La Guma does not make a distinction between writing a short story and writing a novel. He sees his task to be similar to that of the African storyteller, namely that of recording events as told to him and fashioning the tale in such a manner that there is both a moral and an entertaining purpose involved. La Guma observes that "I begin the story at the beginning and bring it to its end when all has been told" (2). As in the novels, the stories rely heavily on narratives that had been told to the writer or on events with which he had been personally

involved. Many of the stories on South Africa were
conceived during periods when La Guma was in jail or
under house arrest and they reveal in theme the sociopolitical concerns he experienced then. Several of the
stories were created simultaneously with some of the
novels and at times characters and themes of the stories
and the novels coincide. Hence La Guma's aim, as will be
discussed later, in A Walk in the Night and And a
Threefold Cord to portray the history of the Cape
colored community is very much present in the action and
theme of many of ths stories. The characters are invari-
ably colored and the problems evoked, though part of the
general tragedy of the South African scene, are more
relevant to race relations between coloreds and the other
racial groups of the country.

    In an article called "Form and Technique in the Novels
of Richard Rive and Alex La Guma," Bernth Lindfors aptly
summarizes the style and theme of La Guma's work as
follows:

> La Guma's style is characterized by graphic descrip-
> tion, careful evocation of atmosphere and mood, fusion
> of pathos and humor, colorful dialogue, and occasional
> surprise endings. His stories most often concern law-
> breakers—criminals, prisoners, prostitutes and
> apartheid offenders—who possess either an unusual
> sensitivity or a sense of honor or morality which
> redeems them as human beings and raises them to heroic
> stature. These slum-dwelling heroes are victims of
> their environment and their passions. When they act,
> they do not exercise their own free will but rather
> they react to the pressures and forces working on
> them from within and without. (3)

If one examines carefully the first two stories that La
Guma wrote, "Out of Darkness" and "Nocturne," one will
appreciate what Lindfors means.

    "Out of Darkness," like "Tattoo Marks and Nails" and
The Stone Country, shows La Guma's personal experience
both with prisoners and with the condition of life in
South African prisons. The story, told by Old Cockroach
to the narrator, "is actually a true one no matter how
bizarre it sounds" (4). The reader does not discover
until the end of "Out of Darkness" that the story's main
theme is the practice of "play whiteism" and the tragic
result that emanates from this practice. The fact that

the theme of the story does not appear until the end does
not weaken it. In fact, it allows the writer to create a
tale of interest and suspense that may otherwise have
suffered in the telling of the story.

The story occurs in a prison cell where the chief
protagonist, Old Cockroach (Ou Kakkelak), the narrator,
and several prisoners are locked up. Since the story
begins with a recognition of the sharp "smell of unwashed
bodies and sweaty blankets" and the description of "the
heat in the cell" as being "thick as cotton wool" (5),
the reader does not suspect that the story will transcend
the environment of the cell. La Guma continues to cap-
ture the prison scene, recording the movements, gestures,
and actions of the prisoners and guards. In Smiley
Abrams he also draws for the first time a picture of the
prison bully, a character who plays an important role in
both "Tattoo Marks and Nails" and The Stone Country as
The Creature and Butcherboy, respectively. The reader
learns that in prison little attention is paid to the
weak such as Old Cockroach. Having established the
atmosphere for the story, it is now possible to place Old
Cockroach's gentle insanity in context. Old Cockroach is
in the seventh year of a ten-year sentence for committing
culpable homicide on his friend Joey. Although Old
Cockroach in his "insanity" speaks from time to time to
Joey, the story does not in the first place deal with
this relationship. It needs a prying and sensitively
probing new prisoner such as the narrator to draw the
story out of Old Cockroach. He recognizes that Old
Cockroach is "an educated man [who] might have been a
schoolmaster before he had committed his crime" ["Darkness," p. 33] and by encouraging him to tell his tale of
crime La Guma skillfully leads the reader to the true
purpose of the story.

According to Old Cockroach he had been "a teacher at a
junior school and was doing a varsity course in [his]
spare time" when he met and fell in love with the "beautiful" Cora ["Darkness," p. 37]. He had grown up with Cora
in the Cape colored suburb of Woodstock, properly known
in Cape Town as the chief suburb of the "play whites."
All his life plans, including marriage, were centered on
Cora. But Cora "was almost white" and realized that in
an absurdly racist country such as South Africa one can
benefit from one's light skin. Hence, she frequented
"white places, bioscopes, cafes" ["Darkness," pp. 37-38].
Old Cockroach is "black" and was therefore unable to

take Cora to these places. Cora "drifted away" from him,
but he "kept on loving her":

> I talked to her, pleaded with her. But she wouldn't
> take any notice of what I said. I became angry. I
> wept. I raved. Can you imagine how much I loved her?
> I grovelled. I was prepared to lose my entire self-
> respect just to keep her. But it wasn't of any use.
> She said I was selfish and trying to deny her the good
> things of life. I would have given her anything I
> could. And she said I was denying her the good
> things of life. ["Darkness," p. 38]

The final humiliation to Old Cockroach comes when Cora
tells him "to go to hell," slaps his face, and calls him
"a black nigger" ["Darkness," p. 38].
    Racing ahead the narrator rightfully assumes that it
is at this point that Old Cockroach was forced to "[lose]
his head" and to "kill her" ["Darkness," p. 38]. But the
story ends on a surprising and ironical twist when Old
Cockroach answers as follows:

> Oh no, I could never have done that to Cora. I did
> lose my head, but it was Joey whom I killed. He said
> I was a damn fool for going off over a damn play-white
> bitch. So I hit him, and he cracked his skull on
> something. ["Darkness," p. 38]

As a story of love, jealousy, and honor, there is
enough told by Old Cockroach to give some meaning to the
event. But La Guma's stories tend to provoke rather than
to be final or complete. Furthermore, they require background understanding before full enjoyment can occur.
First and foremost the story is about the overwhelming
South African question of skin color. Cora is in love
with Old Cockroach until she recognizes that because of
her light skin color she can in fact enjoy the privileges
of a world that Old Cockroach cannot provide. The South
African system of racial division is very much predicated
on pigmentation: the lighter the person the better the
socioeconomic privileges. Since a small number of Cape
colored people happen to "look like whites," some of this
group tend to work and to socialize among whites. But to
"play white," as it is known, is a risky business should
the authorities discover the offending types; hence, many
"play whites" leave their colored suburbs for work before

dawn and arrive home after nightfall. They literally carry out their new existence in "darkness." "Out of Darkness" refers to this literal journey from a "dark" (colored) suburb to a white world in the darkness and also to what is believed to be personal journeys of dark people from darkness into whiteness.

A prerequisite for this risky existence is the untying of previous attachments to the colored world the "play whites" come from. This very often includes a denial of family members when confronted accidentally during the light of day. Seeing the new, enjoyable privileges offered by her skin color, Cora becomes disenchanted with Old Cockroach even though he works extremely hard and is prepared to offer her a stable and happy married life. Unable to convince Old Cockroach of her attraction to her new life-style, she uses the most powerful and humiliating argument against him. She criticizes his dark color, and La Guma shows that it is only in an absurdly racist country such as South Africa that remarks like those of Cora's can actually demean Old Cockroach.

Although "Out of Darkness" is only La Guma's second published story, the surprise ending shows that he knows already how to use suspense and irony to sustain the reader's attention. And yet the ending serves as more than a storytelling device. Old Cockroach's blow against Joey, which accidentally leads to his death, is ironical in two ways: it is the already humiliated Old Cockroach who in defending the honor of a "play white" worthless girl causes Joey's death and receives the further humiliation of a prison sentence; and Joey, who recognizes the cruelty that has been inflicted unfairly on his friend, must die because he speaks the truth. And the greater irony (and moral of the story) is that the system of racism that creates this tragic happening continues in its destructive way with little hope of being defeated.

"Nocturne" reveals La Guma's strength in creating atmosphere, portraying character, reporting dialogue, using contrasts, and, once more, amplifying the surface meaning of his story so that the reader can suggest further possible meanings. According to the writer, "the story was originally called 'Etude' and grew out of my love for classical music and my frequent visits to the Cape Town City Hall to hear the orchestra play" (6). On the surface level the story is simple and direct and contrasts the reality of the life of the chief protagonist, Harry, with the desire he harbors in his soul.

Harry is one of a group of three who are planning to rob a factory. The plans for the robbery are discussed with Harry by Frog and Moos at a bar, the Duke's Head. But Harry's attention is caught by music emanating from a piano across the street from the bar and not by Moos's explanation of the robbery strategy. He continues to concentrate on the beautiful sounds wafting into the open windows of the bar. He is especially interested in "Nocturne No. 2, in E flat major, by Chopin" (7), and when he leaves the bar he is attracted to the building where the music comes from. He finally enters the room and is invited by the girl who is playing the piano to sit down and to request pieces to be played. He persuades her to play the Chopin piece again. But the "old clock on the sideboard" ["Nocturne," p. 115] catches his eye and he remembers his robbery date with his companions. Before leaving, however, he is invited to return on another day. Although Moos and Frog are furious at Harry for being late, his mind is wrapped up with the sound of the music and the sentimental thought "that it would be real smart to have a goose [girl] that played the piano like that" ["Nocturne," p. 116].

What seems like a fairly straightforward story dealing with the ugly facts of a robber's life contrasted with the enchanting music supplied by a lovely girl is in reality an intricate eye-opener on the South African sociopolitical situation. Undoubtedly the contrasts between beauty and ugliness and between imagination and reality dominate the story. For Harry, deprived of a proper education and "a chance to listen to his kind of stuff" (classical music) ["Nocturne," p. 115], the real world is the one he shares with Moos and Frog planning and executing robberies to survive in an unfair society. His humdrum world is in the Duke's Head. Although reduced to being a part of this hopeless, depressing setup, Harry is sensitive enough to respond to the chords of beautiful sounds and he can, therefore, ignore the insistent strategy instructions of his friends and permit his mind to wander. As he leaves the pub he is still partly absorbed in the world of music and he finds himself drawn to the building where the music comes from. In the earlier passages La Guma portrays the beautiful world of music in an exquisite and enchanting manner. This beauty is now contrasted with the ugly reality of the world that Harry survives in, the hopeless poverty of the people who inhabit the building from which the music

originates, and the awful-looking building itself. The
music comes to Harry "like a spring of cool water in a
wasteland" ["Nocturne," p. 113]. But Harry is still part
of the humdrum world and he is surprised to discover that
the piano player, with her face that is "dark and fine
and delicate" ["Nocturne," p. 114], is interested in the
beauty of the music for its own sake and not for money,
as Harry assumes everyone to be. Although entranced by
the music, he cannot leave the world of robbery and violence, and the old clock on the sideboard brings him back
to a world he knows best. He can, therefore, only see
the world of music as lovely and unreal and to be enjoyed
only when he has time for it. He continues to regard
this world as one for the "High bugs [who] go to the City
Hall to hear it" ["Nocturne," p. 115] and, hence, he
would like a "goose" such as the piano player not for the
reality of the music she represents but for her show-off
value.

In "Nocturne" the careful and realistic drawing of the
Duke's Head pub with its "quiet" atmosphere in the "afternoon" and its frantic activity at "six o'clock" give the
reader a good feeling for the story's atmosphere. The
use, and perhaps sometimes overuse, of simile and metaphor to draw the environment of both the music and the
ugliness of the people and the building are well developed. Through Harry's absorption in the music the reader
can see that there is more to Harry's character than
simply being a robber. Hence, when Harry claims that he
was deprived of such music because of his poor upbringing, the reader shows sympathy and even wonders aloud
whether if he had been given "a chance to listen to this
kind of stuff" ["Nocturne," p. 115] he may not have ended
up as a robber. But La Guma persuades the reader to be
realistic enough to accept that the social environment
contributes much to the protagonist's behavior. Even the
piano player, though housed in poor surroundings, has
been fortunate enough to receive training in a convent.
And now to show her gratitude she entertains the dispossessed and from time to time they are captivated by
beautiful strains of music as in Chopin's "Nocturne" and
allow themselves the luxury to dream and to transcend
their dismal environment. But South Africa's racist
ugliness is for the moment more powerful, and it succeeds
in depriving people such as Harry of enjoying fully the
beauty of music and transforms them instead into robbers.

The questions in regard to the value of classical

music in a collapsing community, the enigmatic presence
of the girl and her neat musical room, and the lasting
influence of music on Harry's world need some explora-
tion. Typically, because there are few answers and many
questions, La Guma uses a title and provides a story that
leave the reader unsatisfied and questioning. It is not
commonly expected that in an oppressed community there
would be the presence of classical music. But it is one
of the ironies of the racist division of South Africa
that within a community such as the Cape colored there is
a small but significant class stratification at work.
Hence there will be some coloreds who have been given an
opportunity to learn to play classical pieces on the
piano and others who have attended symphony concerts at
the City Hall. For these few the naming of Chopin's
music is not out of context at all. But in being followers of classical music they also claim for themselves,
arrogantly, a certain class superiority over types such
as Harry and the "scarred saints" of the dilapidated
building.

The piano player's role is of particular interest. In
one way she is completely honest in what she is trying to
do: that is, she has a learned skill and sees her playing as a form of missionary role of bringing momentary
escape to people who have been discarded by the larger
society. And as some people do walk into her room to
listen and others inside and outside the building are
enchanted and given a short time of escape, she seems to
be successful in her mission. But the questioning of her
mission comes in regard to the atmosphere she creates and
even in the musical offerings she presents. Her "neat,
dustless, [and] polished" room is in striking contrast to
the general decay that surrounds her, thus being a
valiant form of defiance; it is the presence of the
"framed music-school certificates hanging with Queen
Victoria" on the "papered walls" ["Nocturne," p. 114]
that strike the reader's curiosity. As kind, generous,
and honest as the girl may be, she cannot help but contrast herself with the people who listen voluntarily or
involuntarily. This witting or unwitting stance and the
playing of musical pieces (however enchanting they may
be) that are not recognizable by her audience remove the
player from her audience and create in them the feeling
of an unreal, escapist world. In this sense, then, the
music is much like the "beer and port" that drug Harry,
Moos, and Frog and fire up their courage to plan the rob-

bery of a factory. When the robbery is over, the robbers
will have to return to their real world of brutality and
racism. Their ill-gotten gains will help them to return
to the pub to escape into the unreal world of alcohol.
Someday, however, they will be arrested and the reality
of South Africa as a stone prison will confront them.
So, too, for Harry and the others, the music is a tran-
quillizer that numbs their deprived and dispossessed
senses just long enough before the brutality of apartheid
confronts them.

Both "Out of Darkness" and "Nocturne" deal with
moments of escape from the brutal racist reality of South
Africa. This theme is prevalent again in "A Glass of
Wine" and "Slipper Satin." Both stories deal with the
controversial issue of the Immorality Act of South Africa
and show racism in a menacing and soul-destroying way.
In "A Glass of Wine" a "tall and young and thin as a
billiard cue" white boy with "beautiful red-gold hair
combed in a high pompadour" (8) comes to Ma Schrikker's
house to court her brown daughter, Charlette. Ma
Schrikker is the owner of an illegal drinking establishment, known in the ghetto as a shebeen. La Guma remembers Ma Schrikker as "a real-life character, fat and
jolly" and at whose "shebeen I enjoyed many happy
moments" (9). In fact, originally the writer considered
"writing a story about Ma Schrikker alone" (10).

Also present on the occasion of the white boy's visit
is the narrator and his friend Arthur. After imbibing a
fair amount of red wine, Arthur enquires from the white
boy whether he is in love with Charlette and whether he
plans to marry her. Arthur continues in this questioning
vein until he is forcibly ejected from the shebeen. Once
on the outside, Arthur asks the narrator in a puzzled
manner, "What they get so funny about?" ["Glass," p. 96].
The narrator replies as follows: "You and your wedding.
. . . You know that white boy can't marry the girl, even
though he may love her. It isn't allowed." Arthur
responds to this revelation by uttering, "Jesus. What
the hell" [ibid.]. The use of both "Jesus" and "hell" in
one breath sums up in a contradictory but devastating way
one aspect of racism in South Africa. Since the invasion
of South Africa in 1652, there has always been some form
of mixing between couples from the white and nonwhite
communities. This interracial mixing is in large part
responsible for the origin and growth of the Cape colored
community. With the advent of Afrikaner power and the

fanatical teachings of the Dutch Reformed Church the
argument that the white race is being weakened by the
joining of blood between the blacks and whites has become
strident and menacing. Soon after assuming power in 1948
the ruling Nasionale party enacted the notorious "Immorality Act," which strictly forbids sexual relationships
between whites and blacks. The legal penalty for violating this law is either a stiff fine or prison sentence
or both. But since such an action is frowned upon by the
majority of both the white and black communities, the
guilty participants, especially the white ones, tend to
commit suicide rather than be put to shame in an open
court trial. Suicidal deaths, family break-ups, and
mental disorders have been counted in the thousands since
the enactment of the Immorality Act.

Even to contemplate the absurdity of a practice that
forbids a normal love relationship, one must see it
through the eyes of inebriated people. Hence, the whole
discussion occurs while the narrator, Arthur, and the
white boy are consuming red wine. In his unsteady state
Arthur can pose questions about the love relationship,
which will normally be hushed up by both communities.
But even in such a licensed state the participants and
the bystanders are embarrassed and finally force Arthur
out of the shebeen. In both "A Glass of Wine" and
"Slipper Satin" La Guma is concerned about the reaction
of the colored community because a law is effective only
inasmuch as it is willingly supported by those who are
victimized by it. Outwardly in "A Glass of Wine" the
love of the white boy and Charlette is tolerated and
accepted in an unassuming and even humorous way. Both
the narrator and Arthur comment on the boy's looks and
manners and show general approval of his courtship. They
encourage Ma Schrikker to summon Charlette to the drinking room so that the lovers can be together. Arthur's
bantering tone in observing the love relationship is
good-natured and his logical conclusion that such public-
ly displayed love must clearly end in blissful marriage
is logical everywhere but in the absurd world of
apartheid South Africa. Arthur is therefore rightly
offended when he is asked to leave the shebeen because of
his "sacrilegious" utterance.

In "Slipper Satin" the colored community is not as
approving of Myra's situation. The story opens with Myra
returning from prison, where she has been for four months
for violating the Immorality Act. Her white partner,

Tommy, fearful of the exposure to his community, killed
himself before he could be taken to the police station.
Myra is now exposed to the disgrace and humiliation of
her own community, which comes from three sources. First
there are the "idle men" who watch her and smile gently
at her "conquest" (11). Second are the womenfolk who
peer shyly at Myra as she passes by them and then break
into loud, abusive chatter. Third is the cold reception
Myra receives from her mother:

> "You brought disgrace on us," her mother said harshly,
> the spoon waving in the girl's face. "We all good and
> decent people, but you brought us shame." The face
> crumbled suddenly and tears seeped out of the eyes.
> "You brought us shame. You couldn't go and pick a boy
> of your own kind, but you had to go sleep with some
> white loafer. You brought us shame, after how I
> worked and slaved to bring you up. Nobody ever been
> to jail in our family, and you a girl, too. It's
> enough to give an old woman a stroke, that's what it
> is." ["Slipper," p. 69]

Myra pleads with her mother that her relationship with
Tommy was a loving one free of color considerations. "It
wasn't any disgrace, Ma. It's no disgrace to love a man,
no matter what colour he is or where he comes from." But
her mother viciously responds that "it's no better than
being a whore" ["Slipper," p. 70].

Myra's intention in returning to her community is to
start life anew. As she walks to her family residence
she resolves not to be bitter any longer. But the gossip-
ing of the unforgiving female neighbors and the cruel
scorn of her mother now force her to recognize that her
punished action was to leave a permanent scar on her
life. Hence, in a resigned, bitter mood she echoes her
mother's accusation of her being a whore: "'All right,'
the girl said bitterly. 'I'm no better than a whore.
All right. Leave it like that. I'm a whore and I brought
you disgrace'" ["Slipper," p. 70]. Although Myra's
sister, Adie, shows her compassion, Myra knows now she
will receive no help from her mother or her community to
rehabilitate herself. The stigma that Myra carries dooms
her to nonmarriage and the likelihood of unemployment.
Hence, when Adie informs her that she would like to have
a satin slip for her wedding, Myra reassures her that she
will obtain it for her. The story ends with Myra certain

that she can "earn eight guineas easily" ["Slipper," p.
73] by prostituting herself.

Unlike "A Glass of Wine," where Charlette's mother
approves of her courtship with the white boy and the
shebeen drinkers encourage the love relationship, in
"Slipper Satin" the womenfolk of the community and Myra's
mother act as a vicious vigilante force that destroys the
chief character. In this regard, then, the Immorality
Act works devastatingly well because large parts of the
community are prepared to accept the absurdity of its
strictures.

"The Gladiators," though seemingly about a boxing
match between a black and a colored South African, takes
the reader back to the theme of "Out of Darkness." In
the latter story the question of "play whiteism" cropped
up and one observed how important skin pigmentation was
in the racist division of South African society. It is
generally assumed that color discrimination occurs only
between whites and blacks, but this is not true, as indicated in "The Gladiators." Just as whites enjoy socioeconomic and political privileges that are superior to
those of any of the other three racial groups in South
Africa, the colored community, being lighter in skin
color than the blacks and Asians, enjoy more socioeconomic privileges than the other two nonwhite groups. As in
the case of the whites, many members of the colored community assume an arrogant attitude toward the blacks and
Asians and can see these groups in a contemptuous light
only.

The reader learns in the opening paragraph of "The
Gladiators" that Kenny, the colored boxer, "just miss[ed]
being white" and that this is the chief reason for his
being "so full of crap" (12). Kenny's racial arrogance
creates uneasiness in his second. The first remark from
Kenny confirms the second's view: "I'll muck that black
bastard." And when the trainer reminds him that "we all
blerry black, even if we off-white or like coffee," Kenny
dismisses his reasoning by wondering, "But what the hell
I got to fight black boys and coloured all the time."
Since competitive sport between whites and nonwhites is
prohibited in South Africa, Gogs and the second inform
Kenny that he would have "to go to England" or "Lourenco
Marques." Insisting that his opponent "ain't our
kind" ["Gladiators," p. 115], Kenny enters the boxing
ring.

Even before the fight is properly underway Kenny

dismisses his opponent as a tsotsi ("street thug") and
boasts that he will beat him. But in the fourth and
fifth rounds the black boxer begins to take command of
the fight. Kenny, however, in his racist delusion
refuses to admit the skill and power of his opponent and
thus dismisses the advice of his corner man by reiter-
ating that his opponent is a "black piece of crap" that
must be pounded into "hell." In disgust the corner man
shakes his head and indicates that he is "leaving this
blerry play-white penny-ha'penny braggard alone after
this" ["Gladiators," p. 119]. Kenny is not able to withstand the further punishment that the black boxer metes
out and he is finally knocked out, with his "face a mess
and his mouth swell[ed] up like a couple of polonies"
["Gladiators," p. 120]. In such a state of disfigure-
ment, Kenny is unable to boast any longer of his racial
superiority. But there is, of course, no guarantee that
the racial prejudice he displayed earlier will leave him.

The narrator is also concerned with the crowd at the
boxing match and any transformation that may occur. The
crowd is predominantly colored and thus tends to favor
the colored boxer Kenny. When he enters the ring the
crowd "shout themselves hoarse for Kenny," whereas the
"good-looking boy with a dark, shiny skin and thick
chest" is not given "a big hand" and is in fact laughed
at in derision when he warms up. Somebody in the crowd
later refers to the black boxer as "kaffir" and urges
Kenny to "[d]onder" (beat) him ["Gladiators," p. 117].
The narrator wonders about the country he lives in, where
the evil spread by the racist regime has infected so many
of the oppressed that they are ready to accept the
pecking-order of skin color. While Kenny is successful
both the racism of the crowd and its natural instinct for
blood are satisfied. When the black boxer takes command
of the fight, however, the crowd forgets the racist
distinction of skin color and yells "for the black boy to
give it to" Kenny ["Gladiators," p. 118]. The crowd is
transformed completely into just another boxing audience
when Kenny is savagely conquered.

"The Lemon Orchard" and "Coffee for the Road" deal
with events that actually occurred in South Africa: the
threat of racial violence that occurs when members of the
oppressed groups finally refuse to accept the injustices
of the apartheid system. "The Lemon Orchard" is based on
the savage beating of a colored rancher in the rural town
of Calvinia in the Cape. The teacher had charged the

minister of the Calvinia Dutch Reformed Church with
assault, "and as this was regarded by the Afrikaner community as an unheard of affront to God's servant by a
Hotnot" the teacher was taken at night from his home and
"beaten up savagely" (13).

La Guma's story keeps the main outline of the actual
event; but instead of simply concentrating on the blood-
thirsty act that is to occur, he emphasizes more subtly
the atmosphere of sterile, brutal racism tinged with the
fertile, fragrant growth of a lemon orchard. Here, as
earlier in "Nocturne," he displays the excellent ability
to contrast human ugliness with nature's beauty and creates an authentic climate in which a terrible deed is
to be enacted. The story deals with the kidnapping of
a black teacher by several white men because he, according to the leader of the group, "had the audacity to
be cheeky and uncivilized towards a minister of our
church and no hotnot [derogatory term used by whites to
denote coloreds] will be cheeky to a white man while I
live" (14). The reader is told further by the leader of
the group that

> the amazing thing about it is that this bliksem should
> have taken the principal, and the meester [minister]
> of the church before the magistrate and demand payment
> for the hiding they gave him for being cheeky to them.
> . . . This verdomte [stupid] hotnot. I have never
> heard of such a thing in all my born days. ["Lemon,"
> p. 135]

"The Lemon Orchard" gives the reader an excellent
demonstration of how La Guma portrays the brutality of
South Africa. In ironical, understated language, tone,
and action ominous hints are given of the fate that the
teacher is about to suffer at the hands of five white
men. The title itself is clouded in irony. The lemon
fruit is a bittersweet citrus variety and the smell it
gives off is sharp and pungent. The beating that the
teacher is to receive is to occur in the lemon orchard,
where the "fragrant growth" and "the pleasant scent of
the lemons" ["Lemon," pp. 135-36] contrast sharply with
the bitterness of the human deed. Pleasant as the
orchard may be it is also "a small amphitheatre"
["Lemon," p. 136] where the human hyenas are to devour
the victimized slave to ensure that apartheid's authority
is not challenged.

As in And a Threefold Cord and Time of the Butcherbird, La Guma uses nature's power to identify with human
action very well. It is late winter and the early darkness and chill of the season fit in well with the cold-
ness of heart and darkness of purpose of the victimizers.
In the first paragraph the moon, as if ashamed of what
she is to witness, hides "behind long, high parallels of
cloud." The vile-intentioned men can also be seen, but
their shoes sink "into the soil and [leave] exact, ridged
foot prints." Again, as if aware of the dreadful event
that is to occur, the "crickets had stopped their small
noises" and a dog which started "barking in short high
yaps . . . stopped abruptly" ["Lemon," p. 131].

The human hyenas, however, do not stop in executing
their dastardly deed. The writer captures them aptly
when he observes that they are dressed in hunting clothes
of "khaki trousers and laced-up riding boots, and an old
shooting jacket with leather patches on the right breast
and the elbows" ["Lemon," p. 132]. They stalk and soften
their prey by abusing the man both physically and mentally. Physically they press the muzzles of their shotguns
"hard into the small of the man's back above where the
wrists" meet and by "striking him on a cheekbone" ["Lemon," pp. 133-34]. Mentally they call him derogatory
names such as "kaffir," "hotnot," "bastard," "verdomte,"
and "donder." His education is detested and he is
referred to as an "educated hottentot." He is also
called a "black Englishman" since he can speak English
better than his tormentors and because some rural Afrikaners believe that educated blacks were trained by
English-speaking whites to oppose them.

The violence in the human mind is, however, not
carried out without a witness. As the victimizers lead
their sacrificial lamb to the slaughter in the amphithe-
ater of the lemon orchard, "the chill in the air
increase[s]," "the creek-creek-creek of the crickets"
creates a "high-pitched sound," and the moon comes out
"from behind the banks of cloud" while "the perfume of
lemons seem[s] to grow stronger, as if the juice was
being crushed from them" ["Lemon," p. 135]. But the
racist tormentors of the black teacher are oblivious of
the external signs and regard the lovely, forbidden
orchard "as good a place as any" to carry out their vile
deed. As so often in other works of La Guma, the story
ends with nature expressing the hope and defiance of the
oppressed: "The moonlight clung for a while to the

leaves and the angled branches, so that along their tips
and edges the moisture gleamed with the quivering shine
of scattered quicksilver" ["Lemon," p. 136]. Once again
a terrible injustice is acted out; but once more there is
indication that this kind of injustice will not continue
forever.

"Coffee for the Road" demonstrates well how the writer
uses his personal experiences and those of other people
in his work. According to La Guma, "this true story was
narrated to me by an East Indian South African woman.
I, of course, created the atmosphere, dialogue and so
on" (15). The story demonstrates a vast and intimate
knowledge of the semidesert Karoo. "This knowledge,"
says La Guma, "came to me when I and others were detained
in 1955 in a small Karoo town. I also made use of this
knowledge when I wrote Time of the Butcherbird" (16).
As in most of La Guma's stories, the climactic moment is
short and intense as the tired and harried chief protagonist of the story in frustration hurls a thermos
flask at a white serving woman. But to arrive at this
point, the writer provides the reader with many intimate
and informative details of geography, racial division,
and human frustration.

The chief protagonist, a "dark, handsome, Indian
[woman] " (17), is driving the family automobile from
Johannesburg to Cape Town, roughly 1,000 miles. The
three-day journey is in its second day when the chief
incident occurs. Accompanying the woman is her whining
and restless six-year-old daughter, Zaida, and her slightly older son, Ray. The woman would have preferred to
make the long, arduous journey by train, but her husband,
Billy, "had written that he'd need the car because he had
a lot of [business] contacts to visit." She had driven
throughout the night because she "was determined to
finish the journey as quickly as possible." But, because
of the racist situation in South Africa, there are no
hotels available for nonwhites and thus by the early
morning "she was fatigued, her eyes red, with the feeling
of sand under the lids, irritating the eyeballs" ["Coffee," p. 86]. To add to her misery, she has to tolerate
the unhappy, pestering Zaida, who is unwilling to take
care of her own puny needs and desires. At the insistence of Zaida she decides finally to pull up outside a
café on the main street of a rural Karoo town to seek
coffee. As in the case of hotels, the Afrikaner-
dominated rural areas have no cafés where nonwhites can
sit down to enjoy food and refreshment. All that is

available to nonwhites is "a foot-square hole" in "the wall facing the vacant space" of the café where, at the point of the woman's arrival, has assembled in a line "a group of ragged Coloured and African people [who] stood in the dust and tried to peer into it, their heads together, waiting with forced patience" ["Coffee," p. 89].

The woman refuses to join the humiliating line and proceeds to walk confidently into the café, where the only customer present is "a small white boy with tow-coloured hair, a face like a near-ripe apple and a running nose." The serving woman, who is described as having "a round-shouldered, thick body and reddish-complexioned face that looked as if it had been sand-blasted into its component parts," is surprised and stunned by the presence of a nonwhite person inside the "whites-only" café and screams in disgust at the woman when she asks that her "flask" be filled with coffee ["Coffee," p. 90]. Although startled by this "screeching," insulting outburst by the white serving woman, the Indian woman's years of suffering humiliation at the hands of whites suddenly reaches the breaking point and, while accusing the white woman of being "bloody white trash," she hurls her thermos flask in "disgust" at the white woman, striking her forehead and causing her to bleed. As she storms angrily out of the café, her actions and brisk movement are "stared" at in disbelief by the ragged collection of nonwhites on the outside. She leaves the depressing town, vaguely aware that repercussions will occur. White policemen, complete in "riot-truck" and "holstered pistols," are given orders to set up a roadblock on the highway and to arrest the woman. When they finally arrest her, she is accused of being "one of those agitators making trouble here" and assured in harsh tones, "You make trouble here then you got to pay for it" ["Coffee," p. 93].

This story of the cruel heartlessness of South African white society is played out against the backdrop of the harsh geography of the Karoo. Here again La Guma shows how the atmosphere of nature can be used effectively to describe human behavior. The realistic and beautiful description of the Karoo anticipates the longer passages of Time of the Butcherbird. The opening description of the Karoo in the first paragraph of the story anticipates the magnificent beginning of the novel. La Guma refers to the "semi-desert country that sprawled away on all sides in reddish brown flats and depressions" ["Coffee," p. 85]. Like the sterile racism that exists in the human

world, here, too, the "miserly earth" is infertile and
"scattered with scrub and thorn bushes, like a vast
unswept carpet." It is a land of "flat country and dust-
coloured koppies, the baked clay dongas and low
ridges of hills" with a "landscape ripped by, like a film
being run backwards, red-brown, yellow-red, pink-red, all
studded with sparse bushes and broken boulders" ["Coffee," pp. 86-87]. This hostile land is now occupied by
the Afrikaners, who are unhospitable toward nonwhites,
forbidding passersby a place to sleep at night, a café
to eat in during the day, and concealing the blacks "in
tumbledown mud houses" ["Coffee," p. 86].

Certain that the status quo will last while the nonwhites in the Karoo are browbeaten, the Indian woman's
behavior, like the "funny bird" Ray sights (later to be
known as the butcherbird), is regarded as revolutionary;
hence she has to be punished and reminded of her inferior
position. In this way, then, "Coffee for the Road" is
much like "The Lemon Orchard" and promises the oppressors
in South Africa that the oppressed have not resigned themselves to their ignoble position.

The apartheid system influences the behavior of all
South Africans, regardless of color or nationality. And
often the cruel aspects of racism are reinforced by class
behavior. This is especially true in the story "At the
Portagee's," which seems slight at first glance. Once
again the reader is transported to the District Six world
of A Walk in the Night and taken into a shabby café
owned by a Portuguese to witness both race and class
discrimination. Before one can understand the nuance of
action and sullen look that emanate from the owner of the
café it is necessary to appreciate the class and race
standing of the Portuguese. La Guma uses the Afrikaans
word "Portagee's" to describe a person who has emigrated
to South Africa from Portugal or former Portuguese
African colonies such as Angola, Mozambique, and Guinea-
Bissau. The Afrikaners by history and practice tend
not to accept strangers easily into their midst. Two
factors, however, have forced the Afrikaners to accept
reluctantly the influx of immigrants from Europe since
the Second World War. The first is the fear that the
blacks will outnumber the whites by such a large margin
that the whites will be defeated by numbers alone.
Second, South Africa's industrial expansion has meant
a greater need for skilled labor, and since blacks are
not permitted to hold skilled jobs it is necessary for

the regime to import whites from abroad.

But in true Nazi fashion the regime has tried to import immigrants from northern European territories with the expressed belief that their Protestant and Nordic qualities will make them fit in better with the Afrikaners. But when this intention could not be fully met, the regime was forced to accept immigrants from Catholic and southern European countries. Hence, both in religion and in their darker complexion immigrants from these countries have been barely tolerated by the Afrikaners. People from this area, and in this story a "Portagee's," usually find themselves living in suburban areas that border the nonwhite suburbs. Furthermore, many of them tend to be shopkeepers (a position that relegates them to the economic and social lower middle class) who own cheap shops in the nonwhite areas. The goods they sell and the appearance of their shops tend to be of low quality. The café in the story is described vividly as serving "steak and chips," "egg roll[s]," "coffee," and "fish" and the tables are often bedecked with "empty Coca Cola bottles." It smells of "cooking," with the "fried bacon and boiled vegetables and coffee" giving off a stale aroma. The ceiling has attached to it "streamers of fly-paper" and it contains a jukebox where noisy music can be heard (18).

The café owner's appearance is in keeping with the shabby sweatiness of the place. He is described aptly as a "very fat Portagee" who wears "a greasy apron around his belly" and who has a "red sweaty" face ["Portagee's," p. 111]. Although like Mostert in And a Threefold Cord and Barends in Time of the Butcherbird the Portuguese owner is dependent on the nonwhite consumers, he displays utter contempt toward his needed clients. His racist behavior toward the colored customer who does not have enough money to obtain food is an indication of two neuroses from which he suffers. First, he accepts the racist policies of the regime, and as his credentials are not fully accepted in the Afrikaner community he has to demonstrate with severity his loyalty to the system. Second, although loyal to the regime he is not fully accepted into the white society; hence he shows his frustration (and supposed superiority) by being rude to all his black customers, but especially to those who give him a reason to react.

The black man is described as "thin and dirty," with his "face covered with a two-day beard." He is dressed

in "an old navy-blue suit that was shiny with wear and
grease" ["Portagee's," p. 109]. Since the state of the
café and the appearance of its owner resemble more closely the place and the look of the black man, it seems
unjust that the owner would become belligerent and insulting when the man orders a sixpence portion of fish. The
owner in a vicious manner responds, "You can't get sixpence food here, you bladdy fool," and after threatening
to remove him from the café by physical force he calls
him a "loafer" ["Portagee's," p. 111].

When the narrator, Banjo, and Hilda and Dolores leave
the café, the sullen owner refuses even to recognize
those who patronize his establishment and ensure his
comfortable, privileged existence. In this short sketch
of South African life, La Guma has succinctly expressed
the view that although the privileged whites cannot survive without the blacks, they try to live as if the
blacks were nonexistent or nonhuman. Furthermore, he
indicates that the immigrant whites, often rejected by
the early settlers, tend to judge the measure of their
success in South Africa by how effectively they can apply
the system's strictures to the underprivileged of the
country.

In "A Matter of Taste" La Guma shows that regardless
of the racist laws of South Africa, which seek to destroy
harmonious communication between the races, there is a
natural propensity among human beings to share their joy
and despair. This gives reason for both hope and pessi-
mism: hope reveals itself in the fact that the races can
cooperate and aid each other; but this hope threatens the
racist governors of the system and causes them to create
more laws that can prevent cooperation. The story deals
with two black men who have "just finished a job for the
railways" and a scruffy, hungry white man who harbors
dreams of working on a boat that will "make the [United]
States" (19). The black men are poor and are unable to
afford supper—all that they possess is some coffee,
which they are in the process of boiling "some distance
from the ruins of a onetime siding." When they are ready
to serve the coffee they are surprised by the arrival of
a "thin," "short," "pale white face" man who is "covered
with a fine golden stubble." The man's shabby appearance
indicates that he is among the discarded of the white
society and that he has not had food for some time. His
physical condition is clearly worse than that of the
black men. But since he also is a victim of hunger he

becomes one with them. But before a bond can be established among the three men, there are certain practices
of the racist system that must be overcome. Chinaboy,
who first observes the arrival of the white man from "the
plantation," is suddenly and uneasily interrupted in his
task "of pouring the coffee." Chinaboy's unease stems
from the fact that although he and his friend are "camped
out" near an abandoned "one-time" railway siding, whites
are generally suspicious of such occurrences and respond
by arming themselves and then forcibly ejecting the
blacks from the land. Second, his unease reflects his
indoctrinated belief that whites are far too privileged
to appear in the shabby dress of the white man. The
white man is also uneasy: he is not accustomed to
seeking aid from blacks, but his hunger forces him "hesi-
tantly" and hopefully to remark, "I smelled the coffee.
Hope you don' min" ["Matter," p. 126].

In a lesser writer the opportunity to exploit this
delicate moment in a propagandistic way would be ideal.
La Guma, however, deftly weaves his tale so that he may
hint at the unusualness of the encounter but still
continue with his chief purpose: to show that at certain
levels the racist system is also a class system affecting
both white and black. Hence the focus of the story
becomes the common desire of the three men to have a
proper meal rather than the meager offering of a cup of
coffee. The difference in race becomes secondary to
their culinary needs, and even when they refer to each
other in usually contemptuous racist denotations such as
"Whitey" and "boys" they do it more in a friendly than in
a pernicious manner. In a bantering tone Chinaboy
invites the new "table boarder" and the narrator jokingly
refers to the "sparing" of "some of the turkey and green
peas." Chinaboy, after indicating to the "white boy"
that they are not "exactly [at] the mayor's garden
party," begins to long for "a piece of bake bread with
[the] cawfee" ["Matter," p. 127]. This longing by Chinaboy gives rise to a discussion of foods that are not now
available to the poverty-stricken threesome and, once
again, suggests the unreality of their world.

But there is disagreement between Chinaboy and the
white boy in regard to their taste for food. After Chinaboy indicates that "I'd like to sit down in a smart caffy
one day and eat my way right out of a load of turkey,
roast potatoes, beet-salad and angel's food trifle," the
white boy responds, "Hell, it's all a matter of taste.

Some people like chicken and othe's eat sheep's heads and
beans!" But Chinaboy is not convinced and argues, scowl-
ingly, that it is not "a matter of taste" but "a matter
of money" ["Matter," p. 128]. This disagreement does not
affect the camaraderie and soon afterward Chinaboy and
the narrator plan the illegal freight ride to Cape Town
of the white boy. Before he jumps onto the train the
white boy shares his last three cigarettes with the black
men and thanks them "for supper." The embarrassment of
begging coffee from blacks at the beginning of the story
has disappeared at the end when he feels familiar enough
to refer to the blacks as "boys" in a fraternal and non-
racist manner ["Matter," p. 129]. After he is finally
helped onto the train, the white boy raises his hand in
salute to his newfound compatriots. The salute is
returned by the black men, and as if to indicate that
this can become a normal part of South Africa, Chinaboy
wonders, "Why ain't the band playing? Hell!" ["Matter,"
p. 130].

La Guma's conclusions to most of his stories are often
ironical and packed full with thought. In "A Glass of
Wine," as indicated before, the writer has Arthur exclaim-
ing both "Jesus" and "Hell" to describe the absurdity of
the Immorality Act. In "A Matter of Taste" Chinaboy
observes that the bond that has been established among
the threesome seems natural and, therefore, there is no
need to bring out a band to celebrate the occurrence.
But since the regime has convinced many South Africans
that such camaraderie is not possible between the races,
this successful event needs to be trumpeted with fanfare.
When Chinaboy calls out "Hell" he is referring both to
the absurd "Hell" of racism that the country lives in as
well as to the fact that only in a nightmarish society
like South Africa can a normal occurrence between
individuals be considered unusual.

The stories "Late Edition," "A Matter of Taste,"
"Tattoo Marks and Nails," and "Blankets" are anecdotes of
individual interest rather than being in the tradition
till now of seriously examining race relations in South
Africa. These vignettes of life in District Six and in
Roeland Street jail are considered by La Guma to be
"exercises of the imagination and the testing of my
ability to observe and to report interesting anecdotes"
(20). In "Late Edition" the writer concentrates on a
familiar scene in District Six, namely that of a young
boy earning "spending money by selling newspapers" (21).

It is not so much the boy who interests the writer, but
the passersby and the atmosphere of the district. In "A
Matter of Honour," a slight story about a bragging former
boxer and a jilted husband, it is the narrator's sensi-
tivity and kindheartedness and the surprise ending that
preoccupy the writer. The setting of the story is a pub
in District Six where the narrator, his friend Arthur
(who had been previously seen in "A Glass of Wine"), the
ex-boxer, Fancy, and the jilted husband (who is described
as a beggar or "shark") meet. Much of the conversation
is between Fancy and Arthur and consists chiefly of
Fancy's boast that he had through his alleged charm lured
away from her husband a woman named Lily McDaniels. The
ex-husband, who is unknown in this role to the other
drinkers, finally tires of Fancy's boasting, and although
he is bloated, drunk, and clearly outmatched he challenges Fancy to a fist fight. He is badly beaten but he
sees his challenge as necessary. The narrator, who is
angry at Fancy for having beaten a drunk man, is left in
a mystified state when the drunk, with a grin, informs
Arthur that "it was a matter of honour like" (22) as the
ex-husband to fight the man who had taken away his wife.
Since this revelation is cleverly concealed until the
last paragraph of the story, the writer is able to evoke
the sensitive, emotional thoughts of the narrator as well
as to relate an incident that carries with it much
interest.

The "punch line," so to speak, of La Guma's stories
often appears at the end of the story. The writer has a
penchant for surprising or astonishing endings, and, as
in the case of "A Matter of Honour," "Tattoo Marks and
Nails" also concludes on a surprising note. This story
was told to La Guma while he spent several months in
Roeland Street jail in 1963. From this period of incar-
ceration came The Stone Country as well, and it is in
"Tattoo Marks and Nails" that the reader is first introduced to Butcherboy and Yusef the Turk, known in the
story respectively as The Creature and Ahmed the Turk.
Again, as in several of the other stories, there is more
here than the interesting and surprising tale that Ahmed
the Turk tells. La Guma uses the story to describe the
prison cell, the inmates, and, most of all, the meaning
and procedure of the prison "trial."

The story that Ahmed the Turk tells deals with his
earlier experience in the Second World War as a member of
the Cape Coloured Corps in Libya. Ahmed the Turk had

been a "lorry driver" and he had been captured by "some
blerry Eyeties [Italians] supporting the Germans . . . at
the time of the Rommel business" (23). His prisoner-of-
war camp was the open field surrounded by "barb-wire
fence with guards walking round and round it all the
time." Since it is the "solid" heat in the cell that
causes Ahmed the Turk to remember his prisoner-of-war
days, he describes the unbearable heat of the camp as
being worse than the cell ["Tattoo," p. 100]. This observation, coupled with the prison "trial" that was taking
place in another part of the cell, leads Ahmed the Turk
to discuss both the "trial" and his reason for keeping on
his shirt.

He notes that although it was desperately hot in the
prisoner-of-war camp, the prisoners were permitted a
"half-a-cuppy a day" ["Tattoo," p. 101] of water only by
their captors. Since this was clearly not enough, one of
the prisoners suggested that the prisoners play a card
game where the winner would be awarded all "the water
reshun." With his "pack of cards, old, dirty, cracked,"
the prisoner was able "to win the whole pot every day,
day after day" ["Tattoo," p. 102]. After a while the
losers became suspicious, and when they examined the deck
of cards they noticed that it was marked. At the "trial"
held by the prisoners the offended had his chest tattooed
with the words: "PRIVATE SO-AND-SO, A CHEAT AND A
COWARD" ["Tattoo," p. 104]. This tattooing resulted in
the fact that the offender could not again remove his
shirt in public without showing his shame. Since Ahmed
the Turk has never removed his shirt, the narrator assumes that he is in fact the culprit.

While Ahmed the Turk tells his story, he is interrupted constantly by the "trial" of a new prisoner that
The Creature and his henchmen are interrogating concerning the alleged role he played in the death outside of
prison of The Creature's brother, Nails. The Creature
had been informed that the person who killed Nails "over
some blerry goose . . . had a dragon picked out on his
chest" ["Tattoo," p. 101]. Since the new prisoner has
such a tattoo, he is now to be placed on "trial" for the
alleged crime. The reader is now informed that the
"trial," which is described extensively in The Stone
Country, is a "common occurrence . . . by the most brutalized inmates, of some unfortunate who might have
raised their ire by bootlicking a guard, or rightly or
wrongly accused of giving evidence against, squealing on,

his fellow prisoners, or having annoyed them in some other way" ["Tattoo," p. 99].

Confessing to the narrator that he "never did like these prison trials" ["Tattoo," p. 105], Ahmed the Turk intervenes on behalf of the newly arrived prisoner. Infuriated and maddened by this rude interruption, The Creature turns his attention to Ahmed the Turk. He accuses him of never having removed his shirt in prison regardless of the heat and challenges him to do so, so that he can see if Ahmed the Turk is the "juba [fellow] with stuff [the dragon] tattooed on his chest" ["Tattoo," p. 106]. For a moment the narrator thinks that finally he will discover whether Ahmed the Turk had been the offender in the Wadi Huseni camp. But Ahmed the Turk's laughing and sneering attitude as he unbuttons his shirt gives the impression that he in fact had not been the prisoner on trial at the camp.

In the story "Blankets" (24) La Guma details to some extent the life of the unfortunate drunk and bully Choker. By highlighting moments when Choker used certain types of blankets, the reader is given insight into his life. And in "Thang's Bicycle" (25), which was written in 1975 when La Guma first visited Vietnam and when the war with the South Vietnamese and the United States was close to its end, La Guma shows that it is not difficult for him to write stories of interest and concern about situations that are different from those in South Africa. His characteristic qualities of creating atmosphere, portraying character, designing realistic dialogue, and fashioning an interesting and imaginative tale are all very much present here. The reader finishes the story more aware of the devastation in Vietnam and appreciating the roles that both humans and machines played in the struggle against the forces of South Vietnam and the United States.

Chapter Three
The Reporter at Work:
A Walk in the Night

A Walk in the Night was published in 1962 at the
University of Ibadan, Nigeria, by Mbari Publications.
According to Alex La Guma, he "really had no hope for the
book. I just did it as an exercise for myself and I was,
therefore, surprised when it went through the way it did"
(1). In 1960 La Guma had been acquitted on the charge of
treason brought against him and 155 others by the state
in 1956. In March 1960 thousands of black South Africans
protested peacefully against the Pass Book Law and in
brutal retaliation the South African police gunned down
sixty-nine people and injured hundreds of defenseless
black women and children in Sharpeville, just outside
Johannesburg. A few weeks after this event the racist
government declared a state of emergency when an unsuccessful attempt at assassination was made on Prime Minister Verwoerd. The state of emergency allowed the
government to arrest thousands of its opponents, and
among these was La Guma. Fortunately, A Walk in the
Night had been completed, needing minor revisions only.
Before entering jail, La Guma had instructed his wife,
Blanche, to forward his manuscript to Ulli Beier of Mbari
Publications. The manuscript, however, was kept deliberately at a South African post office for one year and
Blanche La Guma was fortunate to retrieve it. It was
passed on to Beier when he made a personal visit to South
Africa in 1961.

A Walk in the Night is La Guma's first attempt at
writing "a long story" or novelette as it has since been
called (2). Until the writing of this work, he had written a few short stories as a natural consequence to the
type of reporter's work he had been doing for New Age
(3). In A Walk in the Night and the stories that
precede the novel, La Guma shows characteristic elements
of the work he did as a reporter and columnist for New
Age. A major part of his work was to report on the
happenings at night in the notorious black slum of Dis-

trict Six. Like all ghettoes, District Six is a picture
of rundown, decaying houses and makeshift tin shanties.
It is overcrowded and life teems in its great variety of
hope, despair, love, and hate. Its very overcrowded
nature makes it a perfect place for the fugitive from the
law, but the squalor, the illicit sex and liquor outlets,
and its outlawed gambling dens attract to District Six
some of the shadiest and most aggressive types. Hence,
in these conditions life is acted out in all of its fearful forms. For the reporter of events as they unfold in
District Six or even for the artist who desires to record
a part of the history of a cruelly enslaved people, La
Guma was provided with a tailor-made opportunity to
measure and record the pulse and rhythm of his own
community.

As indicated earlier, his weekly column "Up My Alley"
reported on the many happy, sad, tragic, and bizarre happenings that occurred in District Six. Often he would
use the column to attack the Cape Town City Council,
which was responsible for the maintenance of the district, and the South African government for its failure
to provide decent living facilities for the inhabitants
of the district. He saw this failure of the two govern-
ments as a major cause for the creation of slum conditions and of the growth of violent groups within the
community. In a column titled "The Dead-End Kids of
Hanover Street," published on September 20, 1956, he
gives us a dismal portrait of District Six and shows how
such conditions give rise inevitably to the dissatisfied
and violence-oriented youth of District Six:

> From Castle Bridge to Sheppard Street, Hanover Street
> runs through the heart of District Six, and along it
> one can feel the pulse-beats of society. It is the
> main artery of the local world of haves and have-nots,
> the struggling and the idle, the weak and the strong.
> Its colour is in the bright enamel signs, the neon-
> lights, the shop-fronts, the littered gutters and
> draped washing. Pepsi Cola. Commando Cigarettes.
> Sale Now On. Its life blood is the hawkers bawling
> their wares above the blare of jazz from the music
> shops. "Aaatappels [Potatoes], ja. Uiwe [Onions],
> ja," ragged youngsters leaping on and off the speeding
> trackless-trams with the agility of monkeys; harassed
> mothers getting in the groceries; shop assistants; The
> Durango Kids of 1956; and the knots of loungers under

the balconies and in the doorways leading up to dim
and mysterious rooms above the rows of shops and
cafes.

La Guma concludes this particular column with a dire
warning from both himself and the "Dead End Kids":

> Hanging around and waiting, slums, disease, unemploy-
> ment, lack of education, the terrible weight of the
> colour-bar which withholds the finer things of life—
> all help to grind them down until many of them become
> beasts of prey roaming an unfriendly jungle. (4)

The columns that La Guma wrote on "The Dead End Kids"
and on other happenings in District Six show two characteristic elements that become the motivating force for
the writing of A Walk in the Night. First, La Guma
does not see himself as a mere reporter of bare, surface
facts for a newspaper; instead he is the concerned reporter who desires to probe beyond the surface and to
search out the underlying causes that transform ordinary,
good-natured people into "beasts of prey." Second, in
studying and recording the pulse of his community, he
sees himself in the role of social historian.

The ostensible motivation for A Walk in the Night is
attributed by La Guma to "a short paragraph" he read in a
Cape Town newspaper reporting "that a so called hooligan
had died in the police van after having been shot in
District Six" (5). La Guma did not investigate this
particular incident but, as he says,

> I just thought to myself how could this fellow have
> been shot and could have died in the police van? What
> happened to him? And so I sort of created the pic-
> ture, fictitiously, but in relation to what I thought
> life in District Six really was like. And so I wrote
> the sad story, A Walk in the Night. (6)

La Guma's remarks raise several questions about the
system of news reporting in South Africa. Through
monopoly and many unfair laws South African news media
are totally controlled and managed by white South Africans. The result of such control means that only stories
that have direct or indirect links to the white populace
receive proper attention. The happenings in the black
community are of newsworthy interest only when these

events touch the existence of the white community or whenever something of a particularly bizarre nature occurs
within the black community. Even then the white reporter
does not make a serious investigation of the incident and
is quite content to rely on second- and third-hand
accounts of the happening. Furthermore, since South
African society is divided rigidly along lines of race,
the white reporter is often unfamiliar with the terrain
he has to scout and ignorant of the pulse and rhythm of
the black communities. Hence, in the case of the story
that gave rise to A Walk in the Night, the reporter of
the short blurb had simply copied out the daily police
report and left it to his editor to use as filler. La
Guma, in his role as reporter and member of the community
from which the "hooligan" originates, recognizes the
superficial work of the white reporter, and in writing
his own fictional account he demonstrates how the
reporter should have approached his work.

To understand the "hooligan" it is necessary to be
aware of both his personal and communal history, especially since both he and his community have been victims of
an abnormal, racist society. A chief aim, then, is to
give the reader a clear view of the Cape colored community and what is expected of them:

> One of the reasons why I called the book A Walk in
> the Night was that in my mind the coloured community
> was still discovering themselves in relation to the
> general struggle against racism in South Africa. They
> were walking, enduring, and in this way they were
> experiencing this walking in the night until such time
> as they found themselves and were prepared to be citi-
> zens of a society to which they wanted to make a con-
> tribution. I tried to create a picture of a people
> struggling to see the light, to see the dawn, to see
> something new, other than their experiences in this
> confined community. (7)

In the sense, then, that La Guma describes his purpose,
A Walk in the Night concerns itself with the social,
economic, and political purpose of the Cape colored
community and this is further confirmed by the writer's
affectionate dedication of the book to three colorful
Cape Town characters with whom he grew up (8).

The developing consciousness of the colored community
is depicted through the development of many major and

minor characters and through the setting of District Six.
First there is Michael Adonis's gradual movement from
being a law-abiding citizen to the desperate position of
being a "skollie," or local thug. Second, the novel
studies the development of the lives of Willieboy and
the "skollies" and shows how inevitably the unfair racist
system forces law-abiding people such as Adonis to join
either the dissolute ranks of Willieboy or the world of
underground violence and crime and the "skollies."
Third, through the study of the perverse police work of
Constable Raalt, the reader is given an insight into
the objectives and modus operandi of the South African
white police. Last La Guma describes the conditions
of living of District Six and demonstrates clearly
why the lives of the various characters develop as they
do.

The development of consciousness in Michael Adonis is
closely tied to the racial problem in South Africa and
the social environment that exists in District Six. District Six embraces three types of youth: the law-
abiding, eager-to-work citizens such as Michael Adonis;
the deliberately and chronically unemployed such as
Willieboy who eke out an existence by becoming wards of
their working friends; and those, like the "skollies,"
who choose crime and violence to finance their expensive
drug and leisure habits. Since the world of capitalist
investment and work creation is entirely in the hands of
the white community, the eager-to-work youth must make
contact with the white community. Often, however, the
black workers are treated with contempt by better-paid
white workers, and as there is no redress for the gratui-
tous insult from white workers the black worker learns
either to cower to the insult or he challenges his
tormentor, which inevitably leads to his losing his job.
Many of the challengers would then go on to search for
new jobs and often have the earlier experience repeated.
Some of them in frustration and resignation would finally
join either Willieboy or in a fit of vengeance the
criminally oriented group. The story of Michael Adonis,
which preoccupies La Guma in A Walk in the Night, is a
tracing of this scenario.

The characters in A Walk in the Night, as is true of
most of the characters La Guma uses in his stories and
novels, are "actual characters" La Guma knew or observed
as both an inhabitant of District Six and as a reporter
of events in that area:

In terms of material I think I'm one of the fortunate people who has got ability to recall things which appear obscure to other people but registers with me as being useful in creating a picture so that most of the description of action or places in District Six is based upon actual characters and events. I used this information and connected events in order to create the whole picture. (9)

The character of Michael Adonis, according to the writer, is modeled after many youths in District Six, but, in particular, Daniel, a childhood friend of La Guma's:

I've seen many boys like Adonis growing up in Cape Town. When I was a young boy I had a close friend named Daniel and we used to play together on the street. But because he was considered black we were separated from each other by the Group Areas Act. Many years later, when we had both grown up, I met Daniel again—but only now he had become a gangster, a street corner hooligan with a pretty bad reputation. And as he had once been my childhood pal, it moved me very much. I was really taken up by the fact that we had each gone our divergent ways. Daniel had been one of the characters of my youth who had made an impression on me. There were others like him who had gone to school with me. Not that they necessarily ended up as criminals. Many of them remained ordinary people living in a state of despair, not knowing where to go, but just living one day to the other, trying to earn a living. These are the real characters of A Walk in the Night. (10)

The story of Adonis begins when he literally drops "from the trackless tram" (11) and falls into the reader's consciousness for over ninety pages. Adonis is not as yet ready to enter District Six because he has not resolved the angry question that has haunted him since he walked away from his place of work earlier that day. Adonis had lost his job because he had challenged one of the white workers who had insulted him. He describes the incident to Willieboy as follows:

That white bastard was lucky I didn't pull him up good. He had been asking for it a long time. Every time a man goes to the piss-house he starts moaning.

Jesus Christ, the way he went on you'd think a man had
to wet his pants rather than take a minute off. Well,
he picked on me for going for a leak and I told him to
go to hell. [p. 4]

Willieboy, who belongs to the group of the chronically
unemployed, provides Adonis with no encouragement by his
insistence that work, and work for any race, is a foolish
choice: "Me, I never work for no white john. Not even
brown one. To hell with work. Work, work, work, where
does it get you? Not me, pally" [p. 4]. When Willieboy
continues in his nonchalant manner to deride those who
work, a mixture of anger and resentment springs up in
Adonis "for a fellow who was able to take life so easy"
and who in the process did not have to face the insults
of the white community. Michael Adonis is, then, offered
an alternative life-style, but one he is still too defiant to accept. There is still the matter of that "sonavabitch, that bloody white sonavabitch" [p. 5], which he
vows to avenge.
      One of the ways to avenge his white tormentor is to
join the "skollies." The "skollies" are the thugs who
believe in living well by robbing those who are affluent
in society. They, too, had at one time been eager-to-
work citizens and, like Adonis, had been insulted. So
instead of meeting their tormentors face to face in the
light of day, when so-called legitimate law was at work,
they chose instead to meet their tormentors at night,
when their violence-ridden methods provided them with
superiority. Moreover, since their aims included financial gain, they found themselves in a much better position than if they were to have pursued their aims at the
white man's workplace. The "skollie" option is presented
to Adonis at the same café where he has met Willieboy,
but at this early stage he considers the "skollies" to be
"a hardcase lot" and even "the anger over having got the
sack from his job had left him then, and he was feeling a
little better" [p. 7].
      This feeling, however, is soon dissipated when Adonis
confronts the next stratum of white society, the police.
Here La Guma takes the opportunity to observe that blacks
have only two ways of contacting the white community:
one is through the workplace, where blacks work for
whites; the second occurs when blacks meet up with the
white police force, which tends to patrol, often in a
brutal and perverse manner, the ghettoes of South Africa.

South Africa, La Guma believes, is a veritable police
state. Both as a reporter and as an activist opposer to
the unfair, racist laws of South Africa, he had many
opportunities to observe the South African police at
work. In all of his books there are a variety of descriptions of the South African police. In A Walk in the
Night he describes the police as follows:

> Michael Adonis turned towards the pub and saw the two
> policemen coming towards him. They came down the pave-
> ment in their flat caps, khaki shirts and pants, their
> gun harness shiny with polish, and the holstered pis-
> tols heavy at their waists. They had hard, frozen
> faces as if carved out of pink ice, and hard, dispas-
> sionate eyes, hard and bright as pieces of blue glass.
> They strolled slowly and determinedly side by side,
> without moving off their course, cutting a path
> through the stream on the pavement like destroyers at
> sea. [pp. 10-11]

It is in this guise that the police confront Adonis and
humiliate him by accusing him of being a vagrant and of
using and peddling dagga ("marijuana"). When Adonis
denies these charges he is told in a brutal manner not to
lie and to "turn out your pockets." All of this takes
place in broad daylight and in the embarrassing presence
of people passing by. Unable to lay a charge against
Adonis and in their customary perversion, the police end
the bullying with:

> "Well, muck off from the street. Don't let us find
> you standing around, you hear?"
> "Yes, (you mucking boer)."
> "Yes, what? Who are you talking to, man?"
> "Yes, baas (you mucking bastard boer with your
> mucking gun and your mucking bloody red head)."
> They pushed past him, one of them brushing him
> aside with an elbow and strolled on. [p. 12]

This Adonis considers to be utter humiliation—once again
at the hands of his white tormentors. Hence, "deep down
inside him the feeling of rage, frustration and violence
swelled like a boil, knotted with pain" [p. 12].
    This feeling does not dissipate when Adonis makes his
contact with the third level of white society and accidentally kills the drunken Uncle Doughty. From the time

that the sailors and administrators of the Dutch East
Indies Company arrived at the Cape of Good Hope there had
been sexual contact between the white and black communities. When the Cape colored community became a distinct
group in the racial spectrum of South Africa, many
whites, and in particular those who failed to succeed
economically in the white community or refused to accept
the racist views of their community, drifted over to the
colored community and lived within the racial boundaries
set aside for coloreds. These whites are referred to as
"poor whites" and are often treated with great contempt
by the colored community. Many of them have colored
wives or mistresses and together they are known best for
their drunkenness and for the squalid conditions in which
they live. Uncle Doughty, who claims to have been once
one of the great actors who excelled in Shakespearean
plays, is an Irishman who emigrated to South Africa,
lived with a colored woman, and now ekes out an existence
in a filthy room situated in the same building in which
Adonis lives. According to La Guma, Uncle Doughty is
modeled after "an Uncle who lived in District Six":

> He was an old man who had been an actor and found him-
> self living in a room in District Six. He was found
> dead one morning by his landlady. So I used this in
> order to complete the picture. In fact, I might con-
> fess that he was a relation of ours--he was my
> mother's second cousin or something like that who had
> landed up in District Six with no place else to go.
> He had taken a room and he was a little degenerate old
> man, continually drunk, but nothing could be done with
> him anyway. He became a party to the scene. And then
> one day he was found dead in his room. (12)

It is Uncle Doughty who invites Adonis into his room
to "have a drink" from a bottle of port he purchased with
his "old age pension." Adonis responds angrily against
both Uncle Doughty and the humiliation that whites had
caused him by rejecting Uncle Doughty's offer and by
reminding the old man that "Youse not my uncle either
. . . I haven't got no white uncles" [p. 25]. But Adonis
helps the drunken man into his room and "with a sudden
burst of viciousness tossed the wine down, then [flung]
the glass back into the old man's lap" [p. 26]. Uncle
Doughty, sensing Adonis's vicious mood, informs Adonis
that "we all got something to worry about. . . . We all

got our cross to bear." Adonis's response is placed in a
racial context when he insists that Uncle Doughty has
nothing to cry or worry about because he is an "old white
bastard." In reply to Adonis's contempt, Uncle Doughty
expresses the theme of the book when he says both white
and black are "like Hamlet's father's ghost" [p. 27] and
goes on to recite lines from Shakespeare's play to illus-
trate his meaning:

> "I am thy father's spirit, doomed for a certain time
> to walk the night . . . and . . . for the day confined
> to fast in fires, till the foul crimes done in my days
> of nature's . . . nature are burnt and purged away
> . . . But . . ." He broke off and grinned at Michael
> Adonis, and then eyed the bottle. "That's us, us,
> Michael, my boy. Just ghosts, doomed to walk the
> night. Shakespeare." [p. 28]

Adonis rejects this description of his position and in
his own intoxicated state he blurs his vision of the
white worker who had insulted him with that of the
drunken, white "old bastard" and avenges himself by
striking "the bony, blotched, sprouting skull" [pp. 28-
29] of Uncle Doughty with the bottle of port. It is the
finding of the murderer of Uncle Doughty that now becomes
the focus of the book.

Adonis's first reaction after the killing is a shocked
awareness of the unpremeditated deed: "God, I didn't
mean it. I didn't mean to kill the blerry old man" [p.
29]. His next reaction is to seek shelter from the law
and to excuse the vile deed. Adonis's tragic irony is
that throughout the story he had been humiliated by the
whites and the specter of revenge had loomed strongly in
his mind. But now that he has in fact received some
measure of revenge, the specter of his humiliation and
defeat becomes an even greater presence to contend with.
If he saw himself as a haunted figure before, his
conscience now makes him doubly haunted and forces him
into a life-style he had not contemplated at the beginning of the story.

He decides that he will not report his crime to the
police because as the white instrument of the law they
would demonstrate no sympathy or justice. After Adonis
makes this decision the dead body of Uncle Doughty is discovered and in the confusion and commotion that follow he
escapes from the building without being seen by any of

the residents. He is unaware that the screaming lady who
discovered the body has in fact seen Willieboy leave
Uncle Doughty's room and, hence, Willieboy is suspected
of having killed the old man. It is, however, the roaming "skollies" who witness Adonis's escape from the building. Before Uncle Doughty's death Adonis had been one of
the unlucky "walkers of the night" whose entire existence
was at the mercy of the white society's whims. Now,
after the death, he is an aimless and haunted walker of
the night whose fear finally leads him to join the true
underground world of the "skollies" and the night. The
stultifying social and political environment leads him
inevitably to the world of crime and perpetual darkness.

Before he decides on his course of crime he meets the
young boy, Joe, who, like Willieboy, is another luckless
member of the deprived community. It is to Joe that
Adonis confides he has "troubles" [p. 65], troubles in a
much bigger category than any of those that the "nondescript boy" may experience. He suddenly recognizes the
importance of his action and assumes a boastful position.
His bravado is met head on by the arrival of the gang of
"skollies" and he is offered a position with them. But
he accepts the offer only after his credentials are
challenged by "the boy with the skull-and-crossbones
ring" and when Foxy, the leader of the gang, informs
Adonis that they had seen him escape from the building
where "a rooker [drunk] got chopped or something" [p.
67]. Adonis feels trapped, and no amount of pleading by
Joe to "leave those gangsters alone" [p. 71] can dissuade
him from his future course. He proceeds to the Hanover
Street Club, where he is welcomed by his mates in crime
and, after he has smoked a few rounds of dagga ("marijuana"), he becomes a full-fledged member of the underground with the prospect of walking the night until he is
arrested or he dies.

In tracing the development (or, in a normal society,
the regression) of an ordinary person such as Michael
Adonis, La Guma gives the reader a vivid and tragic view
of the type of destruction that a radically organized
society such as South Africa can impose on law-abiding
citizens. Furthermore, the writer demonstrates here that
if and when Adonis is arrested or dies, the reader should
be cautious of police or media reports, which provide a
mere summary of the event and ignore the depth of life
that is being reported on. This observation can also be
made in the case of Willieboy, who in fact closely resem-

bles the description in the Cape Town newspaper that
originally inspired La Guma to write <u>A Walk in the</u>
<u>Night</u>. And, like Adonis, Willieboy is modeled after one
of the characters from La Guma's boyhood:

> He's a typical picture of one of the boys in my neigh-
> borhood. He used to be a friend of mine who grew up
> with me. He was among the boys who taught me to play
> the guitar when I was a youngster. On the street-
> corners. And he used to call me professor because
> perhaps I was a little bit ahead of him. (13)

The story of Willieboy serves two chief purposes: it
provides an insight into how unfairly the South African
police system works and how innocent people such as
Willieboy can become victims of the unfairness; and by
tracing the aimlessness and hopelessness of Willieboy's
life La Guma shows why Michael Adonis rejects this pattern of existence and chooses instead that of the underground "skollies." The reader first encounters Willieboy
at a café Adonis has entered soon after his dismissal
from his job. Willieboy is described as an unemployed
young man who sees himself as "always" taking life "easy"
and who has decided that it is not worth working for
either whites or blacks because work in itself is a
useless and perverse exercise. He, furthermore, prides
himself on the fact that he is able to survive by living
off the generosity of others, and it is in pursuit of
this aim that he is drawn to the building where Adonis
lives. Adonis, however, afraid of being discovered,
refuses to open his door when Willieboy knocks. Willieboy then decides to knock on the door of Uncle Doughty's
room to ask him for money to buy <u>stop</u> ("marijuana").
But there is no reply from the Irishman and Willieboy
decides to turn the knob and look in the room. Here he
discovers "the dead blue-gray face" of Uncle Doughty [p.
34]. Willieboy's response is to slam the door shut and
escape from the scene in the fear of being accused of the
killing. But, unfortunately, he runs into one of the
tenants, who recognizes him, and when she discovers Uncle
Doughty's dead body she is convinced that Willieboy
killed the Irishman. Like Michael Adonis, Willieboy's
hopeless but bearable life of simply walking the night of
poverty in the ghetto is now transformed into a life of
fear and panic as he attempts to run away from the tenta-
cles of the cruel law. Once again, La Guma makes a state-

ment about the racist laws of South Africa. In a country
where one's guilt or innocence is determined by one's
skin color, Willieboy knows that his truthful explanation
of his actions will not necessarily be accepted by the
police. Hence, he flees into the night-world of the
fugitive:

> Willieboy strolled up the narrow back street in Dis-
> trict Six, keeping instinctively to the shadows which
> were part of his own anonymity, and thought with sud-
> den anger: Well, I had mos nothing to do with it.
> They can't say it's me. I found him mos like that.
> But years of treacherous experience and victimization
> through suspicion had rusted the armour of confidence,
> reduced him to the nondescript entity which made him
> easy prey to a lie which specialized in finding scape-
> goats for anything that steered it from its dreary
> course. [p. 48]

Willieboy's first stop in his new existence is the
old, illegal drinking and prostitution hideout of Miss
Gipsy. After some persuasion she offers him a bottle of
wine on credit. At this juncture the room is filled with
the entry of two colored girls and two American seamen
whose boat was stationed at the Cape Town port. Even in
his own morally hopeless state Willieboy is able to distinguish between types of immorality and thus berates the
girls for "messing" around with "foreign boggers" [p.
53]. His remarks are brought to the attention of the
seamen and this causes a physical fight. Willieboy is
knocked to the ground and thrown out of the shebeen (an
illegal drinking place) to continue his life of "walking"
in the night. This embarrassing humiliation leads
Willieboy finally to assess his own position and project
his future aims.

The reader learns from Willieboy's self-examination
that "all his youthful life he had cherished dreams of
becoming a big shot." While he has "seen others rise to
some sort of power in the confined underworld" he has
"found himself left behind." In the gangster movies he
watched avidly he envied "the flashy desperadoes" and
dreamed "of being transported wherever he wished in great
black motorcars and issuing orders for the execution of
enemies." But when "the picture faded and he emerged
from the vast smoke-laden cinema mingling with the noisy
crowd he was always aware of his inadequacy, moving un-

noticed in the mob." To offset this nondescript portrait
of himself, Willieboy

> had affected a slouch, wore gaudy shirts and peg-
> bottomed trousers, brushed his hair into a flamboyant
> peak. He had been thinking of piercing one ear and
> decorating it with a gold ring. But even with these
> things he continued to remain something less than
> nondescript, part of the blurred face of the crowd,
> inconspicuous as a smudge on a grimy wall. [p. 72]

He is, however, convinced that "Hell, I'm a shot, too.
I'll show those sonsabitches" [p. 72]. But his way of
showing himself is in fact mercilessly to beat up the
drunken man Greene.

Willieboy's last act in the story occurs when he finally meets up with the police and is shot. As he tries to
escape from the brutality of Constable Raalt, his mind
takes him back to the broken family life he comes from
and the actions that have finally led him to this fearful
encounter with the police. In providing us with details
of the final minutes of Willieboy's life, La Guma is in
fact answering his own query when he first thought of
writing the story of a "fellow" who had "been shot and
. . . died in the police van." The first portrait that
comes to Willieboy's mind is that of his mother "standing
over him, shouting: 'You been naughty again.'" Here he
recalls that he had used the few pence commission he
received from hawking papers to buy "a big parcel of fish
and chips instead of taking the money home" [p. 83]. For
this and for many other unprovoked incidents he remembers being beaten by his mother. Willieboy also recognizes that his mother's need to punish him physically
grew out of her own resentment at being constantly beaten
by her drunken husband.

Constable Raalt refuses to allow an ambulance to take
the collapsed body of Willieboy to a hospital. Instead,
he insists, "Hell, we'll take the bliksem [bastard] down
to the station. They'll patch him up. He's not hurt so
terribly" [pp. 87-88]. The final pages of the book deal
with the delirious mutterings of Willieboy as he lies
dying in the back of the police van, and in so doing La
Guma is able to amplify the bare police report the Cape
Town newspaper reporter used when relating "that a so
called hooligan had died in the police van after having
been shot in District Six." Still looming strongly in

Willieboy's mind is his mother and her accusation that
"you was naughty again" and the inevitable, consequential
slap on the face [pp. 83-84].   As he thinks of escaping
his pain and going home, Willieboy recognizes that home
means "his father would only beat him again" and desires
rather to go to "the Daffodil Club and play some bil-
liards, or get a drink" [p. 90]. His dismal view of home
is that of being beaten continually and of being "cold"
and "hungry." His death finally comes when in a loud and
clear voice he defiantly announces that "they's always
kicking a poor bastard around" [p. 93].

   Willieboy's life is a tragic path from an unloving
home into a loveless society that finally brutalizes him
to death. As one of the ghosts walking the restless
night, his own being does not surface at all and his
death is a relief from the mindless suffering he has
endured. Willieboy's life is one of the two choices that
Michael Adonis has once he has lost his job.   Adonis,
however, is one of the ghosts who can walk in the restless night and prolong his end by taking the course of
robbery and violence and a life lived off the spoils of
such activities. La Guma does not provide Adonis with
heroic status for choosing this latter way of living.   On
the other hand, in a world where normalcy does not exist
and where one has to confront the underworld of immorality, the life that Adonis and the "skollies" choose is
somewhat better than the hopelessness and pain that types
such as Willieboy must experience.

   La Guma has on several occasions expressed the belief
that South Africa is a police state. In an unpublished
interview he made the following statement concerning the
South African police and the portrayal of the police in
his creative work:

   I believe that in South Africa we live with the
   police. Black people are continually being harassed
   by the police. If it is not for the pass laws it is
   for drunkenness or other social problems. If you read
   the statistics, you find that South Africa has one of
   the biggest prison populations in the world.   The
   police play a big part in the life of the black people
   of South Africa. So that when one is concerned with
   social situations, as I am in my work, one can't leave
   out the police. I think, therefore, that the presence
   of the police in my work is not so much intentional,
   but it is inevitable. (14)

Of the white community that has any contact with the Cape
colored community in District Six, the white police with
little doubt predominate. In the case of A Walk in the
Night, La Guma discusses the role of the police along
two lines: there is first of all the overwhelming power
and brutality of the police as they act as custodians of
the white racist law and seemingly seek to keep order;
and, second, to provide the police system with a human
face, he gives the reader a psychological picture of the
much-hated Constable Raalt—a policeman who was well
known to both La Guma and the inhabitants of District
Six.

The police first appear in the story strolling
"determinedly side by side, without moving off their
course, cutting a path through the stream on the pavement
like destroyers at sea." They have "hard, frozen faces
as if carved out of pink ice, and hard, dispassionate
eyes, hard and bright as pieces of blue glass." In
keeping with their awesome looks and ironclad determination, they view those whom they are supposed to protect
as criminals and speak to them in gruff and intimidating
tones. They inspire a fear in the public so that "only
the very brave, or the very stupid, . . . dared look
straight into the law's eyes, to challenge them or to
question their authority" [p. 11]. And they usually end
their sudden questioning by "brushing," "elbowing," or
cuffing their victim so as to establish fully their
terrifying authority over those they are supposed to
protect.

The insolence and corruption of the white police are
best represented by Constable Raalt. His view of the
colored community and the job of the police is that they
have to ride "around looking at these effing hotnot
[coloreds are referred to in a derogatory manner as
Hottentots] bastards" [p. 31]. On the particular evening
when Willieboy is killed by Raalt, everything seems
"quiet" and it annoys Raalt very much: "I wish something
would happen. I'd like to lay my hands on one of those
bushman [also a derogatory reference to the colored
person] bastards and wring his bloody neck" [p. 39].
Hence, in keeping with his desire, Raalt makes a sudden
raid on the gamblers at the Jolly Boys Social Club.
Raalt is well known to the doorman, Chips, and the other
gamblers at the club. He accepts, illegally, a regular
sum of money so as to permit the club to carry on illicit
gambling. At the club he roughens up the doorman by

striking him across the mouth with the back of his right
hand in order to establish a distance between them. And
when Chips accepts his punishment "without humiliation,
but with a heavy irony in his tone," Raalt strikes him
again "so that the blood formed in a pool in the corner
of his mouth and slid out and down that side of his chin
in a thin, crooked trickle." Raalt finally leaves the
scene after pocketing the "protection money" and after he
has told the gamblers that "you bastards are lucky I'm on
this beat" [p. 42].

Raalt's investigation of the murder of Uncle Doughty
provides the reader with some important insights concerning the attitude of the police toward those they protect
and the reaction of the protected toward the protector.
As seen in the case of both Adonis and Willieboy, there
is a suspicion bordering on fear and hatred for the
police because of the brutal methods they employ and for
the general unconcern and contempt they demonstrate
toward those they are to protect. Hence, when a crime is
committed, as in the case of Uncle Doughty's death, it is
very difficult to find anyone who is interested in providing evidence. Thus when John Abrahams offers to testi-
fy he is referred to by the crowd as a "fif' column" [p.
58]. Raalt enters the building that the dead body is in
after informing the crowd to "eff off" and after brutally
"scattering" the bystanders in the entrance of the tenement [p. 59]. Inside the building he is unable to find
anyone to identify the woman who screamed when Willieboy
left Uncle Doughty's room. Raalt's response to the situation is, "These bastards don't like us; they never did
like us and we are only tolerated here; I bet there are
some here who would like to stick a knife into me right
now" [p. 61]. And when Abrahams continues to provide a
description of Willieboy, Raalt senses the hatred of the
crowd for the police.

Raalt's pursuit of Willieboy is determined and relent-
less, as if failure to apprehend the suspect would be a
blow to his manhood. Hence, once he detects Willieboy,
he stalks him like a hunter, showing no concern for the
curses and jeers of the people in the street. Finally,
when Willieboy is trapped on a roof, Raalt is "quite sure
that he would conclude the hunt successfully" and he
"crouched . . . in the dark and smiled with satisfaction"
[p. 85]. The hunt is ended finally when Raalt shoots his
prey and Willieboy "spun, his arms flung wide, turning on
his toes like a ballet dancer" [p. 86]. The crowd's reac-

tion to the shooting is one of bitter anger but also of
frustration at being unable to prevent the brutality of
the police. Raalt's hatred for those he is supposed to
protect is completed when he rejects his fellow constable's view that an ambulance be summoned to take the by
now dying Willieboy to a hospital, and by his last act of
illegality when he stops at the Portuguese store and
obtains cigarettes without payment while Willieboy's life
is quickly fading away.

There is very little to redeem the police in the eyes
of La Guma and the victims of police authority. But La
Guma desires to give the police a human face and to enter
into the heart and mind of Raalt to see why he acts in
the crude, inhuman way that he does. In other words, the
writer's own bewilderment and his belief in the redemp-
tion of all mankind force him to attempt to rationalize
the brutal actions of Raalt. Some of the blame for
Raalt's actions is placed on the unhappy marital situation that he is in. Raalt suspects his wife of having
extramarital affairs with other men and he is determined
to kill her should he find her in a compromising situation. But since he has not as yet discovered her in a
compromising situation, his home-brewed anger is permitted to ferment and to find release in his brutality
toward those he is supposed to protect in his line of
work. Hence, while on patrol he longs for something to
happen to distract his attention from his marital problems. On the whole, however, this excuse that La Guma
offers for a part of Raalt's behavior is too slight or
too inadequately developed to counteract or even to
explain the overwhelming brutality and hatred that Raalt
demonstrates toward the black community. In the end one
is very much aware that Raalt is an excellent representative of the police state's law and order for which South
Africa is justly notorious.

As stated earlier, one of La Guma's chief aims in
writing A Walk in the Night is to show that the blurb
in the Cape Town newspaper "that a so called hooligan had
died in the police van after having been shot in District
Six" lacks credibility and is woefully inadequate in
illustrating the work that a reporter must do. In
describing in some detail the character and development
of Adonis, Willieboy, and Raalt, the writer goes behind
the scenes and provides the reader with an intensely
agonizing portrait of what occurs in the lives of the
three main characters of the story. La Guma assumes the

character of the reporter he was then and demonstrates in
a painstaking and meticulous manner how a reporter should
carry out his work.   He follows Adonis from the moment
that he steps off the tram, filled with anger, through
his unpremeditated killing of Uncle Doughty, and, finally, to the time when he feels trapped by the event and by
his stultifying environment, which inevitably leads him
to accept the world of underworld activity.   So, too,
does La Guma sketch a portrait of Willieboy: he moves
from his failed and resigned position to one where he
becomes trapped by the police and is finally killed for a
crime that he has not committed.   And in the case of
Raalt, the reader views the activity of the police and
sees how the so-called forces of law and order deliberately contribute to the destruction that visits both
Willieboy and Adonis.   La Guma aims to demonstrate that,
after reading A Walk in the Night, one will never
again accept "short paragraphs" in newspapers as the last
word on events as they occurred.   One will ask the type
of question and seek the kind of evidence that the writer
as reporter presents in the story.

     The novelist's investigation leads him to the conclu-
sion that the people who live in District Six are, like
Hamlet's "father's spirit," "doom'd for a certain term to
walk the night" [p. 28].   In this regard, he sees Adonis,
Willieboy, and Raalt as victims of a perverse social
situation that must inevitably and tragically lead the
chief characters to death or ignoble ends.   From the
beginning of the story the reader is introduced to a
world that can survive only in the unreal and dangerous
atmosphere of the night.   This is a world in which La
Guma grew up and one he knows intimately.   The Portuguese
restaurant's window is "full of painted and printed
posters advertising dances, concerts, boxing-matches and
meetings"; and inside the café, which is decorated with
"ancient strips of flypaper . . . dotted with their victims," the clientele consists of an "unending flow of
derelicts, bums, domestic workers off duty, in-town-from-
the-country folk who had no place to eat except there
. . . and the rest of the mould that accumulated on the
fringes of the underworld beyond Castle Bridge: loiterers, prostitutes, fah-fee numbers runners, petty
gangsters, drab and frayed-looking thugs" [p. 3].   This
is clearly a world where the underdog is ignored and
where he must in the cheap atmosphere attempt to eke out
an existence.   A further portrait of District Six

describes the shabby shopping arcade where "the music
shops" go full blast and where "the blare of records all
mixed up so you could not tell one tune from another";
where the vegetable and fruit hawkers "[yell] their wares
and [flap] their brown paper packets"; where at the bus
stop "a crowd pushed and jostled to clamber onto the
trackless trams, struggling against the passengers fighting to alight"; and where "along the pavements little
knots of youths lounged in twos and threes or more, watching the crowds streaming by, jeering, smoking, joking
against the noise, under the balconies, in doorways,
around the plate-glass windows" [pp. 7-8].

The usual escape for the city dweller who is inundated
with this hard-sell commercialism, shabby exterior, and
neon confusion is the inhabitant's home. But when one
enters the District Six home the squalor and hopelessness
of the interior world dwarf the shabbiness of the
external conditions. The tall, narrow tenement where
Adonis lives was once a Victorian building that "had a
certain kind of dignity, almost beauty," but now "the
wide doorway was chipped and broken and blackened with
generations of grime" [p. 21]. La Guma recalls this
building, or one like it, very well: "In my youth I used
to frequent one of these buildings. I had friends there
and I used to chase after girls" (15).

In the interior of the building the reader is confronted with a "staircase [that] was worn and blackened"
and its old oak bannister is "loose and scarred." The
bulbs of the building, wherever they are in working
order, are "naked," casting "a pallid glare over parts of
the interior, lighting up the big patches of damp and
mildew, and the maps of denuded sections on the walls."
The building "smells of ancient cooking, urine, damp-rot
and stale tobacco" while in one of the rooms "a baby
wailed with the tortured sound of gripe and malnutrition"
[p. 23]. The inhabitants of the building, like Uncle
Doughty, resemble the general squalid conditions of the
tenement. Uncle Doughty has "sagging lower eyelids,
revealing bloodshot rims, and [with his] big, bulbous,
red-veined nose that had once been aquiline, his face had
the expression of a decrepit bloodhound" [p. 24]. The
room he lives in is "hot and airless as a newly-opened
tomb"; the "old iron bed" is "covered with unwashed bed-
ding, and next to it [there is] a backless chair that
serves as a table on which [stands] a chipped ashtray
full of cigarette butts and burnt matches, and a thick

tumbler, sticky with the dregs of heavy red wine" [p. 25]. There is a "battered cupboard . . . in a corner with a cracked, fly-spotted mirror over it," while in "another corner an accumulation of empty wine bottles stood like packed skittles" [pp. 25-26].

La Guma's meticulous description of the squalid and horror-filled living conditions of the disadvantaged prepares the reader for the unpremeditated but mindless violence that destroys the already luckless and dying Uncle Doughty. He concludes that in the underworld of District Six, where the perversely discarded of South African society literally burrows out an existence, it is surprising that there are in fact relatively few acts of violence. In La Guma's view, the external and internal conditions of District Six are responsible for the creation and destruction of Adonis, Willieboy, and the "skollies." And although Raalt and the police must enforce these dismal conditions, they, too, are victims of the ruling society's need to reduce large parts of a voiceless and enslaved people to the role of being perpetual "ghosts" of the night. But in practically all of La Guma's writing there is a note of caution to those who govern the lives of the disadvantaged. In the passage from Hamlet he uses as an epigraph to A Walk in the Night, the last two lines envision a time when "the foul crimes done in my days of nature will be burnt and purged away." And while Willieboy in his final moments of life laments the fact that "us poor bastards always get kicked around" [pp. 84-85], the gathering crowd that watches him being stalked and shot in cold blood by Raalt defiantly observes, "Awright, they'll get it, one day. You'll see" [p. 87]. The conclusion one may draw from this defiant statement, and also from the fact that the community in District Six is solidly against the racist system and the police, is that although La Guma and the colored community deplore acts of violence and immorality, they are acutely aware that, in the night of horror and injustice as described in the story, extenuating circumstances exist to evaluate in a merciful manner the antisocial actions of Adonis, Willieboy, and the "skollies." Furthermore, there is the implicit argument that, when justice does not prevail for a community, the members of that community are not necessarily bound by any of the laws which are responsible for the guidance of that community. Hence, even though the future actions of Michael Adonis cannot be condoned, his decision to join

the "skollies" provides him with a better chance to confront his racist tormentors. To become like Willieboy,
to be a trapped victim of Raalt and the police, is in
fact a denial of the human being's potential for life
even if that life is acted out in the world of ghosts and
damnation. In other words, La Guma finally puts the
weight of the society's evil on those who govern and
those who support the governor. While the governor and
his supporters exert their ill-will on the oppressed, the
oppressed are "doom'd . . . to walk the night" and will
continue to commit "foul crimes."

La Guma's first attempt at writing a long story or
novelette can be regarded as a success. The story has a
clear objective, a fully developed plot, and contains a
welter of incident, character portrayal, and authentic
dialogue to keep the reader's attention. Much has
already been said about the objective and detailed attention that has been devoted to the plot. Apart from the
development of the three chief characters, the objective
of the story is further accomplished by providing addi-
tional vignettes to the plot. The slight portrayal of
the lives of Joe, Greene, Franky Lorenzo, and John
Abrahams amplifies the dismal portrait of the squalid
conditions that are in the main responsible for the
actions of the chief characters. The writer's aim is to
portray the world of darkness existing in District Six,
and each separate insight leads the reader closer to
appreciating the trap in which characters such as Adonis
and Willieboy find themselves. La Guma's chief strength
as a writer is to be found in his ability to portray
character. He is a master at observation, and he does
not fail to notice every line of physique and every
aspect of clothing and posture that a character may
indulge in. By describing the character of Joe, Greene,
and Franky Lorenzo the reader is left with a clear and
deep perception of the lives they live.

La Guma carefully weaves his story around the image of
walking. It appears in one form or another on innumer-
able occasions. From the moment in the first paragraph
of the story that Michael Adonis begins his frustrated
and angry walk through District Six the reader's attention is continuously riveted to the many doomed characters who walk for a while the streets of hopelessness and
despair. As a reporter searching out his story, La Guma
is forced to walk through the district, familiarizing
himself with the everyday detail of the community. As

one who was born and lived in the district, by beckoning
the reader to stroll with him through its streets he is
able to give a meticulous, informed, and poignant portrait of the place and people. This is a place where
there are four types of walkers: the frustrated and
angry, such as Michael Adonis, who are forced to walk out
of their work and into the clutches of the desperadoes;
the aimless and beaten walkers, such as Willieboy and
Joe, who inadvertently become the victims of a cruel
police force; the police, who must patrol the area to
ensure law and order but whose racist hatred causes them
to brutalize those they must protect; and the browbeaten
and weary population at large, who must, like the ghost
of Hamlet's father, walk for a long time the street of
doom, squalor, poverty, and hopelessness. By inviting
the reader to take a slow and careful walk through District Six, La Guma can then pose the question whether the
reader in fact can believe the Cape Town newspaper's
report that a young "hooligan" had been shot and that he
died in the back of the police van. The reader is in
fact left with the overwhelming sounds, smells, and
sights of District Six and a haunting view of a society
and country that, like the ghost of Hamlet's father, must
burn and purge away its foul crimes before the restless
walking in the story will be put to rest. By choosing
the image and action of walking as the chief organizing
metaphor for the story, La Guma not only comments on the
main action that he as a reporter performs, but he takes
the reader carefully behind the scenes and thus ensures
that the reader has an informed opinion of life in
District Six. The reader is thus in a better position to
comment on the problems of South African society and
better able to assess all reports relating to crime in
the black community. In A Walk in the Night, La Guma
strives to develop a compassionate and informed reader,
and in the elements of plot, character, and use of
imagery he succeeds very well.

Chapter Four
The Smell of Poverty:
And a Threefold Cord

And a Threefold Cord was published in 1964 by Seven
Seas Publishers in East Berlin. La Guma recalls that in
1963 he had no particular outlet for his creative work,
and it was during this period that he was approached by
Seven Seas to provide them with "something." In response
to their request, "I offered them And a Threefold Cord,
which they accepted" (1). It is generally said that this
is La Guma's first full-length novel; however, since the
writer does not distinguish between the form of the short
story and that of the novel, one should use the description in a guarded fashion. La Guma's view is as follows:

> Well, to tell you the truth, I had never really
> consciously thought of producing a novel, as such, in
> terms of the formal structures and so on. I just
> started at the beginning and ended at the end. It
> came out that way. I suppose it is necessary to be
> disciplined by certain formulae but it has never been
> something that I have taken specific notice of. I
> just constructed the whole story in my mind, whether
> it was a short story or a long story. I don't call it
> a novel, I call it a long story. Once it has been
> completed in my mind, I sit down to write it and then
> amend it, change it, and so on. But in terms of the
> set formulaes according to which novels should be
> produced, that is never really part of it. (2)

And a Threefold Cord was written while La Guma was a
prisoner in the Cape Town jail on Roeland Street. In
1963 Nelson Mandela, then the leader of the African
National Congress, and several major figures of the
Congress Movement were arrested after spending several
years in organizing the underground military movement
Umkhonto We Sizwe (The Spear of the Nation). Fearful
that a mass, armed insurrection was at hand, the South
African regime arrested hundreds of antiracist leaders

and detained them without charge for varying periods of
time. Since La Guma was an active member of the antiracist Congress Movement, he was detained for several
months, partly in solitary confinement and partly in open
prison. Hence, negotiations for the publication of And
a Threefold Cord were carried out in prison between the
writer and his attorney, and he literally "signed the
contract" there (3).

La Guma provides several motivations for the writing
of the novel. He sees the novel first as being a continu-
ation of what he tried to do in A Walk in the Night:

> Again it is a matter of recording history or recording
> situation. The book is about the suburban slums which
> is a character of the South African scene, whether it
> is Soweto or Alexandra Township or Cooksbush. This is
> just another scene in the life of the community,
> another facet of the picture. I decided again that
> the picture of the suburban slums did not appear any-
> where in South African writing, so I said well why
> shouldn't I do it, because it is part of our life, our
> scene, so it should appear in the picture. (4)

In a later interview he adds the following remarks:

> I was interested in recording creatively the life of a
> community under various conditions. I thought that it
> would help to bring to the reader an idea of what goes
> on in the various black areas of the Cape and that
> through a novel this would be done. And having had
> some experience of the Cape Flats and having met some
> of the people there and having some idea of their
> lives, well I just got stuck into And a Threefold
> Cord. (5)

According to La Guma, he also intended to write a love
story:

> I might add that I thought that at some stage it would
> turn into a love story. It seems as if every writer
> wants to write a love story at some time or another,
> and there is an element of this desire throughout the
> novel. But in general I don't think it is really a
> love story, it is really another record of the general
> life of the people as reflected through the experien-
> ces of one particular family and its associates. (6)

The love story idea is wrapped up with the dedication of the book to Blanche La Guma, the wife of the writer:

> I might have turned it into a love story, but apart from that I think that all the sentiments which are expressed in And a Threefold Cord also have something to do with my wife, Blanche, and our own feelings for the poor and oppressed people. Furthermore, Blanche devoted a lot of her time as a midwife and nurse to working among the poor of the community. So I believe she deserves some mention somewhere. (7)

Another clue to understanding the motivation of the novel is to be found in the title. La Guma describes the title and meaning of the novel as follows:

> The title comes as an excerpt from a biblical quotation. I think it is Ecclesiastes 4:9-12. This excerpt emphasizes the idea that the individual alone cannot survive, that he has to have somebody around him to which to cling in times of difficulty and adversity and I tried to convey the idea that loneliness of people, loneliness of individuals is one thing, but at some time or another they've got to turn away from their loneliness and try to associate with other people. And I try throughout this novel to show that while people have got their own problems, or what they believe to be their own problems, these problems are not actually entirely their own but they are shared by other people. (8)

Brian Bunting, in his foreword to the novel, observes that the book "is drenched in the wet and misery of the Cape winter, whose grey and dreary tones Alex La Guma has captured in a series of graphic prose-etchings" (9). As in the case of A Walk in the Night, La Guma weaves his story around a powerful, unifying, and often directing metaphor. In this case it is the cold and miserable rain that consumes the life and energy of the shantytown dwellers and plays havoc with any dreams they may have. Since nature and the weather play important roles in La Guma's writing, he discusses the use of these elements in the following passage:

> Yes, somebody asked me a little while ago why I always wrote about the weather in South Africa. Well, part

of the fact is that the weather plays a part in creating the atmosphere and it helps to describe the
scenes and so on. There is also the fact that overseas people believe the South African regime's tourist
propaganda that it is a country with perfect weather.
I had an idea that rather we could use the weather as
a feature of South Africa, but also in terms of its
symbolic potential, and thus at the same time make it
or try to make it genuinely South African. In other
words, I am contesting the official propaganda of
South Africa's natural beauty and trying to show the
world that the tourist poster world of wonderful
beaches and beautiful golf links is not the total
picture. (10)

La Guma's storytelling technique of placing characters
against a certain social and natural background is prevalent here as it was in A Walk in the Night. In the
case of the natural context, the writer comments as
follows:

Yes, I try to use nature in terms of symbolic potential and also because the characters have to act
against some background and that background is naturally the slum, the mountainside, or the field. Otherwise, to my mind, the characters would be performing
in a vacuum and would just be making gestures; and
instead of belonging somewhere they would just be
making gestures against a white background and in my
opinion it wasn't enough. (11)

The natural background in And a Threefold Cord rein-
forces the dismal social context the reader has become
familiar with in A Walk in the Night. The reader is
once again confronted with the restless, walking ghosts
of the earlier book and there is a sense that the time
allotted to walk the evil night has not as yet reached
its end. The reporter, now turned social historian, goes
carefully behind the scenes of ghetto existence and once
more places a heavy burden of blame on a racist and class
system that ensures the comfort and luxury of the white
community and relegates the nonwhite community to a
perpetual place of poverty and hell.
     The chief character of And a Threefold Cord, as was
the case in A Walk in the Night, is the socioeconomic
and political environment of the Cape Town slum where the

human action occurs (12). The dreadful lives of the
victims of this environment are examined at a time when
the Cape winter has set in and where the rain has fallen
continuously for days. The reader is made aware of the
woeful slum situation at the very beginning of the novel
when La Guma describes the misery and shabby conditions
of those who inhabit the crowded "pondokkie cabins" and
who must now face the cold rain (13). The world of the
South African slum is one of bare survival, where in addition to corrugated cardboard cartons, rusted sheets of
iron and tin, bitumen and old sacking are also employed
to "stuff . . . into the cracks and joints" [pp. 18-19].

Alex La Guma, as observed earlier, was born in District Six, one of the urban slums on the periphery of
Cape Town. As a child growing up in the ghetto, as a
worker in a factory filled with people from the slum, and
as a political organizer and reporter for a newspaper, he
had many opportunities to appreciate fully the magnitude
of slum life and, as in the case of And a Threefold
Cord, to evoke graphically and intimately the natural
and social decay of slum life. La Guma supports his
authenticity of description and concern as follows:

> Well, I suppose I'm fortunate that, first of all, I
> lived in the slum. I grew up with the people and also
> my political and ideological development allowed me to
> understand them and to identify with them. As you say
> not many see them from the point of the observer. I
> was often involved in the problems of the slum
> dwellers and I think that I might say that I'm lucky
> that I did not confine myself to an ivory tower.
> While trying to write I also participated in and
> shared the problems which the people experienced all
> the time. (14)

Furthermore, he is also able to be both a social worker
and a political activist when he contemplates the slums:

> Possibly other authors have looked at the slums with
> too critical an eye, as simply a blot on the surface
> of the country. They miss the fact that the slum is a
> situation which they grew up in and is, therefore, a
> part which they participated in. I think there's a
> difference between being politically involved and
> being a social worker. The social worker goes among
> the slums and says, "What shall we do about it? It's

such a terrible place," and so on. A politically
involved person is concerned with preventing the slums
from happening again. And I think I'm lucky that I
have been able to combine both roles. (15)

The slum that La Guma writes about in And a Threefold
Cord he identifies as the Cape Town settlement of Winder-
mere, which is separated "like a fortification" from the
white suburb close by. Hence, it serves not only as a
garbage dump of human misery, but is also the dump for
the white suburbanites, so that a part of the settlement
"lay like the back of a decaying monster, its scales of
rotting paper, wood, offal, tin cans and indescribable
filth, heaving and twitching in the stiff, damp breeze"
[p. 45]. The slum has grown through sheer desperation
and in stealth as the harried inhabitants are either
removed forcibly from ancestral lands and property or
they move away from their impoverished rural settings to
the hoped-for material success of the cities. Consequently, with no municipal authorities concerned about the
standard of the structure of house, number of occupants,
electricity, sewage, and health ordinances, the slum
simply grows in a haphazard manner. La Guma's description of the so-called street or lane through which the
slum dwellers wend their way is an excellent example of
the lack of planning in the slum and it gives the reader
a panoramic view of the desperate atmosphere that pre-
vails:

It could hardly be called a street, not even a lane;
just a hollowed track that stumbled and sprawled
between and around and through the patchwork of
shacks, cabins, huts and wickiups: a maze of cracks
between the jigsaw pieces of the settlement, a
writhing battlefield of mud and straggling entangle-
ments of wet and rusty barbed wire, sagging sheets of
tin, toppling pickets, twigs and pealed branches and
collapsing odds and ends with edges and points as
dangerous as sharks' teeth, which made up the fence-
work around the quagmires of lots. [p. 45]

Everywhere in the settlement there is a decaying smell
of "pulpy mould, rotten sacking, rain, cookery, chickens
and the rickety latrines that leaned crazily in pools of
horrid liquid, like drunken men in their own regurgita-
tion" [p. 46] . And in the winter, when life is generally

harsher, "there is no evening" and "the unresisting daylight" is smothered under "its chill, dark blanket." Now
the slum dwellers are forced inside their unbearably
crowded space "where they crouched over puttering oil
stoves, wood braziers or old iron stoves." And while the
slum dwellers huddle close to "the tiny chinks of malnourished light," on the concrete road leading to the
comfort and security of the white suburb the "lights of
high-powered headlamps" coming from "rich automobile
beams" simply ignore "the tumbledown latrines that cir-
cled the listing shacks and shipwrecked people" [p. 87].

Having made the reader fully aware of the external
environment of the shanty town, La Guma now begins to
focus on the decaying structures of the individual shacks
and the large variety of problems that poverty brings.
The shacks in the tenements had been constructed hastily
and with inadequate and inferior materials. Hence, with
their rotten foundations the marvel of it all is that
these shacks still stood for so long against the elements
and ravages of time. The Pauls shack had been built in a
hurry so as to prepare shelter for Ma Pauls, who was at
the time pregnant with her third child, Caroline. Because of their poverty they were forced to make do with
any materials they could scavenge, beg, and steal. The
"warping," "cracking" house was finally built "groaning
like a prisoner on the rack, then settling down in the
face of the seasons with the stubbornness of ancient
ruins" [p. 41]. But the house had not been completed in
time to welcome Caroline into the world, "so Caroline had
been born in a sort of chicken-run which was the only
place where the people who had taken them in had been
able to accommodate them" [p. 39]. And later, when
Charlie and Ronald grew older, "the shack had become too
cramped" and the Paulses "built another room onto the
kitchen, so that now the whole place had the precarious,
delicately balanced appearance of a house of cards" [p.
41].

The shack of the Pauls family is typical of the other
structures in the slum. Hence, by concentrating on the
varying stages of collapse and patchwork attempts to
salvage the shack, La Guma is making a general statement
on housing in urban slums. The house seems in constant
danger of "falling in," and it is only Charlie's constant
care that prevents it from collapsing completely.
Charlie helped his father build the shack, and as his
father's health becomes more fragile it is on Charlie's

shoulders that the responsibility falls for continuing
upkeep of the shack. Hence he is the first to notice the
rain and the leaks it causes in the roof [p. 22]. And
his immediate response to the leak is, "Better fix that
place up in the morning" [p. 24]. In the morning Charlie
walks over to the shabby service station of George
Mostert and asks him for scrap metal with which he
intends to patch the roof. But even as the newly in-
stalled material puts a stop to the leak in the roof,
Charlie is already worried that "the leak would move to
another part of the house, or emerge in several parts"
[p. 80]. The conclusion that La Guma indicates in this
illustration is that, regardless of good intentions and
good will, a shack built on rotten foundations is likely
to continue to deteriorate. Hence, a forlorn Charlie is
left listening to the onslaught of the wind and the rain
as the elements try to devour the poorly built structure.

Although the Pauls shack is typical of most of the
others in the tenement, it is certainly not as bad as the
ones that Caroline and Alfred and Freda and her children
live in. The next best shelter for the poor are the
council houses. These houses are also located around the
periphery of the city and they are built and administered
by the city authorities. They are bare places of existence made up of two rooms and a kitchen with no indoor
hot and cold running water and with an outside toilet.
But they do have electricity and they are constructed
better than the makeshift shacks. But only tenants who
can pay the relatively steep rents are permitted to live
in these miserable houses. And then, too, there is a
long list of people waiting for an opportunity to rent
one of the houses. It is one of the council houses that
Caroline and Alfred had hoped to inhabit but, as Caroline
points out to Charlie, "They reckon we can only get a
house when he get more money" [p. 74]. Lack of money
means, therefore, that the pregnant Caroline and her working husband, Alfred, have to live in the "packing-case
shack" at the back of the Pauls house. This shack is
"small and cluttered" and the couple is forced to sleep
on an "old mattress on the floor." Amidst "a picture of
the Crucifixion in a cracked frame" and that of "a film
star in a cowboy outfit," there is an "old-fashioned oil-
lamp hung from the ceiling" under which Alfy is crouching
"on a rickety apple-box, reading a tattered paperback in
its oily light." In this primitive shack with smells of
"mouldy clothes, smoke and dampness" and through which

"the icy air whistled," Caroline is about to give birth [pp. 146-47]. This fact is regarded as incredible by the white policeman who raids the shack. Even he, hardened by the constant raids of the miserable shacks, cannot understand how it is possible in a hovel with a "smoky ceiling, . . . muddy floor, . . . leak in the roof . . . and ragged clothes" that a baby will be born [p. 150].

There is not much change when La Guma describes Freda's shack. She is found leaning "on the gnarled gate-post before a tiny cabin" [p. 55]. Freda is a widow and the mother of two children dressed in "ragged clothes." The one-room shack has a low ceiling, is cramped, and the "uneven floor of dung and packed earth [is] covered with cheap oilcloth which had worn out long ago." The room has "a cheap kitchen dresser . . . propped against the wall in one corner, and next to it a small table laden with chipped crockery and a primus stove, and a big metal can which held the water that had to be fetched every day from the communal taps." Disrepair and poverty are grimly noticeable everywhere in the room. The "old oval table" has "one of its legs propped with a block of wood." On the table is "a hideous plasterware bowl, its paint cracked and chipped, show[ing] its dirty white insides like scabless dead flesh" [p. 57].

The walls of Freda's shack are "lined with sheets of cardboard from grocery cartons and papered with strips from a printer's dump, so that one could read parts of advertisements and coloured labels as one sat there in the primus-warmth" [p. 59]. The primus, which provides the only warmth for the shack, has one of its legs broken off "and had to be propped up to make it stand." It also works fitfully and Charlie promises to repair it for Freda. As Charlie leaves Freda's shack and she empties the "muddy water" through "the doorway," the reader is left with an overwhelming feeling of the injustice and poverty directed against the enforced poor of the South African slums. Hopelessness abounds everywhere and tragedy must of necessity result.

It is what poverty does to the inhabitants of the slum district that preoccupies La Guma in And a Threefold Cord. The shacks in their varying stages of collapse house inhabitants who because of their crowded, poverty-stricken, and frustrating lives take to cheap liquor, prostitution, family quarrels, and violence. Their already miserable lives are dogged further by sickness, police raids, and the exploitation by the strong among

them of the weak ones in the tenement. They are trapped
in the same manner as the fly whose actions are described
in painful detail by La Guma [p. 82]. The fly "over-
turns" and is now "drowning in the puddle of wine" with
its "angled legs beating the air frantically, its wings
trapped." Unconcerned about the fly's panic, Charlie
wipes "the fly off the box with the side of a hand." The
last view that the reader has of the fly is that of its
falling "onto the floor" and struggling in the darkness
[p. 84].

The inhabitants of the slum are trapped flies who have
been unconcernedly knocked down by the racist and class
system of South Africa, and in their struggling, collapsing positions they are frantically attempting to save
themselves from complete destruction. But the more they
flail and thresh to survive, the more hopeless it seems.
And instead of forming a community to console each other
and to unite against their oppressive situation, the
shack dwellers turn on themselves to seek solace and
satisfaction and to rebuild their destroyed egos. Some
of the shack dwellers see their poverty-stricken state as
God-made and believe that, by trusting in God, things in
time will be set right. Most of these drink themselves
into a stupor so as to forget their miserable condition.
Uncle Ben is of this variety. Uncle Ben, the brother of
Ma Pauls, is described as "a short, tubby man; a dark,
half-burnt dumpling dressed in a holed jersey and shiny,
worn and patched trousers" [p. 76]. He lives "in a
little shack," unmarried, alone, "drinking away most of
the little money he earned doing odd house-painting
jobs." He fears Ma Pauls because she is "against his
excessive drinking and [is] always lecturing [him] about
it" [p. 77]. But he is unable to stop his drinking, as
he ruefully informs Charlie [p. 81]. Uncle Ben recognizes drinking as "evil," as that which makes "a poor old
man" such as Dad Pauls "shiver and shake himself to death
in a leaking pondok without no warm soup and no medi-
cine" and causes him to drink himself into a stupor of
forgetfulness [p. 81].

He is, however, unable to see how the poor can extri-
cate themselves from their trapped positions. He sees
poverty as a natural condition that man must accept and
passively places his "trust in the Lord." Hence when
Charlie suggests to Uncle Ben that "all the stuff in the
world [ought to be] shared," he rejects this notion by
saying it "sounds almost like a sin, that. Bible say you

mustn't covet other people's things." Furthermore, in
his cowed state he spouts out the racist state's slogans that such suggestions are "communis"-inspired and
a way of "talking against the govvernment" [pp. 82-83].
Uncle Ben's threadbare mind is unable to contemplate
the seriousness of his condition; and even though he is
aware that there is an evil responsible for the dreadful
situation that he and others are in, his mind has been
rendered too weak and weary to seek a viable and regenera-
tive way out. Instead, he buries himself in a liquor
bottle, which will inevitably lead to his own impoverished death.

Poverty frustrates Roman as well. But unlike Uncle
Ben, who accepts his miserable situation and then drinks
to forget it, Roman indulges in cheap wine not only to
forget the pain of his condition but to fire himself up
with so-called courage to take out his frustration
through violent acts on others. Roman is a "common
labourer" who drifts from "one mean job to another, earning a few shillings here, a few shillings there." He
lives with his wife and eleven children "in what looked
like an amalgamation of a kennel, a chicken-coop and a
lean-to shed." Despairing about the upkeep of his family, Roman takes to "petty thieving," robbing the weaker
slum dwellers. Occasionally he is arrested and spends
time in jail. Between terms of imprisonment he drinks
heavily, and since, like Uncle Ben, he is unable to identify his real tormentor, the South African race system,
he places the blame for his life of poverty and petty
crime on his wife and his children [p. 103]. Predict-
ably, Roman's response to a situation he cannot properly
analyze is to turn in violence on his family [p. 104].

Roman's regular beatings of his wife lead to hatred
for him and the only connecting link left is the unloving
sexual encounters that lead to monotonous childbirth.
But childbirth in desperate poverty only traps Roman and,
hence, he breaks out in greater violence and turns to
"loose women in the settlement in order to avoid his
wife." But often Roman is rejected by these "loose
women" because "of his wretchedness and poverty" and thus
he returns home to the wife he considers responsible for
his humiliation and beats her up savagcly [p. 105]. It
is the socioeconomic and political environment that has
dragged Roman to such low, violent depths. But until he
is able to recognize this fact, Roman remains a victim of
his environment and turns his anger on the weak and de-

prived rather than on the strong and privileged.

It is the same environment of debilitating poverty
that reduces Susie Meyer to the humiliating position of
being a prostitute. Susie lives in one of the "few old
brick and plaster houses." All that is left of the house
is "a front room and the kitchen" [pp. 96-97]. She has
"a crudely pretty face, the cheek-bones brightened with
rouge, and the lashes too heavy with mascara, the heavy
mouth smeared with glaring lipstick that didn't match her
complexion, and the wiry hair held in a number of plastic
curlers gave her a ludicrous golliwog appearance" [p. 100].
At her youthful age she is characteristically interested
in records and the music of Bing Crosby and in a normal
world where she would be permitted to indulge innocently
in her joint passions of "love and moonlight." But in
the slum settlement where Susie lives she is not permitted to preserve her good looks and youth for a time when
she can be married legitimately and enjoy the normal
interests of life. Hence she uses her attractiveness to
lure men of all kinds. Three of these men are Ronald,
Roman, and George Mostert.

Like Uncle Ben and Roman, Susie is unable to cope with
the overwhelming burden of her poverty-stricken environment. Her need to have "men, men, men"—"Always blerry
men. If it not one is the other one" [p. 99]—is not a
strong or viable response to her stultifying environment.
And as liquor leads the slum dwellers to self-destruc-
tion and death, so Susie's escape into sex and dreaming
music also leads her to destruction. While Ronald
jealously keeps watch outside her residence, Roman is
questioning her about her relationship with "Ronnie
Pauls." Susie indicates clearly to Roman that she
belongs to anyone who is prepared to pay for her sexual
favors, and that includes Ronald. It is in pursuit of
her objective that Susie confronts the poor-white service-
station owner, George Mostert. Mostert's wife has left
him and he lives in lonely and shabby conditions on the
edge of the slum. At the invitation of Charlie Pauls
Mostert has decided on this particular evening to visit
the slum tenement for the first time. Here he is hoping
to find "company and women." But the rain and his lack
of courage force him back to his service station. This
is when he encounters Susie, who offers to accompany him
to his house: "'Ah, I'll come home with you,' Susie
Meyer told him. 'We'll have a little dring, mos. It
isn't so far to your ga-rage'" [p. 128]. Mostert rejects

Susie's offer and she disdainfully dismisses him as "That blerry <u>ou</u> fool. To hell with him" [p. 130].

Ronald Pauls witnesses the scenes with Roman and Mostert, and his immense jealousy causes him to seek redress from Susie. Hence when Susie returns after her encounter with Mostert, Ronald grabs her arm in the dark. He accuses Susie of running after men like Mostert who "got a car and a business and cash." Like Roman, Ronald sees his poverty as the cause for Susie's humiliating behavior toward him. It is Susie's need to taunt Ronald for being poor and for being too young for her that finally drives Ronald into a frenzy of violence and hate. And while Susie gives off "a hideous, ecstatic sound" of laughter "that caught at his nerves like a blunt saw," Ronald pulls out a "half-crown jacknife" and kills her [pp. 144-45]. Susie's hope to escape her poverty-stricken environment by indulging in loose sex and fantasy is thus brought to a tragic end. Once more, a character from the urban slum has attempted to defy the environment, and, once again, the character is mowed down. The tragic lesson to be learned is that the environment is not to be defeated or transcended by turning in on oneself: its defeat is to be found in the united action of the oppressed against the unjust system that created it.

Apart from liquor and loose sex, the dreadful conditions of the slum area further incapacitate the inhabitants by reducing them to illnesses and diseases of various kinds. And when these illnesses and diseases have entered the already undernourished bodies of the inhabitants, they are unable to obtain medical help because they are too poor to pay for the services of physicians. The case of Dad Pauls is illustrated in the novel. It is the inability to obtain medical help because one is poor that Uncle Ben calls an "evil." But Uncle Ben and many of the other slum dwellers who recognize the "evil" are unable to form concentrated action to destroy it. What awaits Dad Pauls, then, is an early death, a death that the poor such as Ma Pauls see as an "act of God" and not the consequence of the atrocious living conditions that the poor must perforce endure. The final dismal sight of a poor person's life is seen at the graveside. While Brother Bombata delivers a "droning sermon," the crowd huddles "around the open grave, among the tombstones, withered flowers, broken jam-jars, the neglected mounds and in-loving-memories and never-to-be-

forgottens" [p. 120]. While this scene is anguished over
the writer reminds the reader that only a small distance
away the white and privileged citizens of South Africa
continue to enact their draconian laws to ensure that
miserable graveside scenes continue unabated.

But the nonwhite poor are not only exploited by the
whites through their system of racism; they are also
victims of crass exploitation operating within the black
community. La Guma illustrates this aspect when he discusses the question of water sales. Water, first in the
form of cold, wintry rain and later to be used to cleanse
the dead, to deliver Caroline's baby, or simply to sustain life, is a major symbol in the novel. Water is
plentiful in a country such as South Africa, which is
surrounded by two oceans and contains countless rivers
and lakes. But for those who live in the urban slums no
water pipes have been laid and water can only be obtained
by borrowing or buying it from "those whose sand-lots had
been laid with plumbing" [p. 113]. When Dad Pauls dies,
Ma Pauls instructs Charlie to "send Jorny-boy with a
bucket" to bring back enough water to "wash down" the
corpse. The cost of such needed water is "a tickey" [p.
108]. Since water is a premium commodity for the poor,
Ma Pauls considers Missus Nzuba's offer to provide her
with water free of charge from her own house as a debt
that must be repaid: "'I'll let you have it back,' Ma
told her. . . . 'I don't want it back, man,' the other
woman said. . . . We all got to stand by each other'"
[pp. 111-12].

But such generous neighborliness does not exist among
all the poor. Those "who owned the plumbing and the taps
sold the water to those who lacked such amenities" [p.
113]. In a cruelly graphic description of a dialogue
between those who have water and those who are without,
La Guma pours all his scorn onto those who exploit others
among themselves:

> "Mister, half a bucket. We only got a penny."
> "Half-a-bucket? Half-a-bucket. Jesus Christ in
> heaven, what the hell must a man do with a penny?"
> "My ma say a tinful of water till tomorrow, mister.
> True as God, mister, till tomorrow."
> "Tell your ma I say tomorrow never come. Tomorrow.
> What you think I am—a blerry millionaire?" [p. 114]

And later, when some of the poor remind their extortionist that they are "all poor people" and ought to help each other, the heartless reply is simply, "Me, I'm poor also. What you reckon I eat? Stones? Grass?" [p. 115]. The South African racist system, which advocates the exploitation of one race by another and thus allows for the extension of exploitation of one person by another, creates cruel divisions within the poor community and destroys compassion. La Guma's sad and inevitable conclusion is that a house so divided cannot marshal enough force to challenge the system that created the disunity. Once again the bewildered among the poor, such as Uncle Ben and Ma Pauls, must accept this further burden as God-made and thus render themselves impotent to change their unjust situation.

The almost unbearable misery of the slum dweller is further compounded by constant police raids. Instead of building a proper settlement for the impoverished, the South African authorities employ large numbers of police who under the name of "law and order" brutalize the already wretched slum dwellers. Under the deceptive guise of searching for those who have violated the pass regulations and those who brew illicit liquor and indulge in smoking dagga ("marijuana"), they literally step on everyone in the settlement in a vicious manner. In the shack where Charlie is sleeping with Freda and her children, the sergeant in charge demands the dagga he suspects Charlie of having. He goes on to cast his eyes lasciviously at Freda in her night clothes and makes open insinuation that her relationship with Charlie is that of a whore. Freda feels, rightfully, that she has been insulted by the constable's insinuation and sobs in deep hurt, while Charlie's frustration at his inability to protect Freda and himself from the "Law bastards" finally forces him to take revenge on his tormentors. In Caroline's shack, where birth of a child is imminent, the policeman is oblivious of the pain and activity in the shack and rudely concludes that drinking is taking place [p. 150]. When informed that a birth is about to occur, even the raid-hardened policeman is unable to believe that birth can occur amidst such awful conditions.

The novel leaves the reader with little hope that things will ever change for the better in the urban slum. Charlie Pauls is the only character who is able to grasp the meaning of the slum dwellers' fate, but he does not possess the force of character to transform the environment in any significant manner. He is, however, as La

Guma points out, "morally and psychologically higher than
the characters in A Walk in the Night" (16). Charlie
is somewhat aware that the dismal living conditions of
the settlement are in large part due to the socioeconomic
and political system of South Africa and the failure of
the oppressed to unite. This awareness is demonstrated
when he narrates to his Uncle Ben a conversation he had
with "a burg working with us on the pipe." "This burg
say, if the poor people all got together and took everything in the whole blerry world, there wouldn't be poor
no more. Funny kind of talk, but it sounds awright."
Charlie reports further that "this rooker say if all the
stuff in the world was shared out among everybody, all
would have enough to live nice." And such a state,
Charlie notes, is only possible when the disadvantaged
and deprived "stick together to get this stuff" [p.83].
It is Charlie as well who dismisses the cause of the
poverty to be that of God's will; nor does he accept the
belief that in God and in the Bible the poor must trust:
"Ma read the Bible every night. It don't make the poor
old toppy any better" [p. 82]. He also dismisses the
deceptive and so-called Christian message of the poor
shall inherit the kingdom of God.

Apart from expressing his awareness of the wrongness
of life in the slums, Charlie does not move in any way to
improve the situation. His only real moment of rebellion
against the unjust system comes when he defies a raiding
policeman and hits him on his "exposed jawbone" and
escapes "into the jungle of shacks" [pp. 141-42]. But
his moment of triumph is shortlived. He must return to
the settlement where the cast-offs of life reside, where
poverty destroys, where family life has been obliterated,
where love turns into hatred because of the overwhelming
burden, where children fantasize away their lives believing they are killers, soldiers going to war, and where
the game of "teckies and burgs" predominates.

The racist system of South Africa is so designed to
reduce the nonwhite community to a place of perpetual
inferiority and sociopolitical deprivation. But the
lessons learned in this type of exploitation are also
applied on a socioeconomic class level within the white
community. This is why La Guma illustrates the case of
George Mostert. Mostert, like his "dirty white" service
station, is cast in the role of a buffer between the
shack dwellers across from his premises and the whites of
the city who race past his service station blissfully un-

aware of his presence. His presence, however, is necessary: without his "lone rearguard action" [p. 64] the
tenement may spread further and finally impinge on the
comfort and security of the white suburban dwellers.

Mostert's wife has left him for another man and now
"over forty years old" he lives in loneliness and misery
[p. 66]. The irony of Mostert's situation is that
"across the road" from his premises he can see the teem-
ing life of the shacks and shanties. Mostert, however,
is white and in South Africa this provides him with a
position of superiority over the shack dwellers and discourages any social contact. The people of the shacks he
sees as being from "a strange country, a foreign people
met only through ragged brown ambassadors who stopped by
sometimes to beg for some useful rubbish, or called a
greeting on their way on some obscure mission" [pp.
66-67].

Yet when Mostert finally converses with one of the
"brown ambassadors," he recognizes a human warmth and a
genuineness of friendship that are totally lacking when
an occasional city white person stops to fill his automobile tank with gas. Although Mostert regards Charlie
Pauls as inferior to himself, he is able to enjoy
Charlie's presence and is attracted to his suggestion of
visiting the slum and having "a party." But Mostert has
over a long period of time been convinced by the racist
system that the people who live in the "bloody dirt and
muck" are inferior to him and thus he sees his decision
to visit the slum as a "desperate adventure" [pp. 71-72].
On the designated "Saturday night" the "desperate
adventure" is begun but not completed. As soon as
Mostert finds himself on the unfamiliar "broken parody of
a street that cut raggedly through one end of the jumble
of shanties," and when he smells the "decaying offal,
rotting wood and latrines"--"the smell of abject poverty"
—he decides "to return to his garage . . . and risk the
sharp hooves of loneliness" [p. 127]. Once again, the
South African slum environment of poverty and the country's racism triumph over human action and force one more
person into a life of loneliness and resignation. Not
making use of a natural ally Mostert is then forced to
come face to face with humiliation from those who are
better off in his own community. This occurs when a
"long, low, smart new station-wagon" is driven up to the
petrol pump. The car is inhabited by a "handsome, pudgy,
artificially-preserved face" woman who is "aglow with

health and complacency" and a "short and plump" man in a
"smart overcoat" whose "healthy layers of fat lay com-
fortably all over him, so that the original lines of his
body were lost in the soft curves" [pp. 160-61].

The woman in particular is bored and shows disdain for
Mostert and criticizes his dilapidated service station.
But when the driver asks about the shack "across the
road," Mostert gladly volunteers the answer that it is
"jus' one of those slum places" and in so doing he
establishes his own superior status over the slum
dwellers and restores a semblance of respectability to
his wounded pride. The driver, however, continues his
brutal criticism of the slum and wonders "why the authorities don't clear the bloody lot out. Just brings disease
and things" [p. 162]. But the driver and his wife are
conscious of Mostert's "dirty place" and they notice his
"grease-lined, broken-nailed hand"; thus in their minds
he is associated with the "muck" and "hell" of the slum.
The final humiliation comes when, "as an afterthought,"
the driver "added a half-crown" as a way of absolving
himself from the poverty and dirt with which he is confronted and to which he has contributed by supporting the
racist, class system of South Africa. As the plump man
switches on his windshield wipers and drives unconcernedly to the north, Mostert watches "the station-wagon out
of sight," shambles back to his office, and before him
"the door of the little glass office waited, as inevitably as the grave" [pp. 163-64].

The socioeconomic and political environment triumphs
over practically every character and initiative in the
book. The weight of the environment reduces the black
community in the slum and the poor white such as Mostert
to a state of inertia and resignation. The indoctrina-
tion that every white South African is brought up with
effectively discourages united action against the tor-
menting system by natural allies such as the poor whites
and the impoverished blacks. And a Threefold Cord thus
leaves the reader with an overwhelming portrait of hopelessness and despair.

Chapter Five
Life in Prison:
The Stone Country

The Stone Country, Alex La Guma's third long book, was
first published by Seven Seas Books in 1967, a year after
La Guma had gone into exile from South Africa. The
novel, however, was written inside South Africa immediate-
ly after La Guma spent five months in jail for being a
member of an "illegal political organization." At this
time the writer was already under a twenty-four-hour,
five-year house arrest order. The novel, says La Guma,
is based

> . . . essentially upon my own experiences and the
> experiences of other prisoners in South African
> prisons. I used the accounts and stories related by
> other people who have been in prison to produce the
> novel. Most of it is completely authentic, but, of
> course, from my point of view. I even personally
> shared the cell with a young boy who is the Casbah Kid
> in the novel. (1)

Hence the novel is rightfully dedicated to "the daily
average of 70,351 prisoners in South African gaols in
1964" (2). This is the year that La Guma wrote The
Stone Country.
     Like A Walk in the Night and And a Threefold Cord,
the chief character of The Stone Country is the socioeconomic and political environment of South Africa, which
creates the conditions of brutality that the major and
minor characters of the novel have to contend with. From
the beginning the reader is made aware that The Stone
Country is about the conditions in South African jails.
Since South Africa's system of racism demands a rigid dif-
ferentiation in every aspect of life, countless numbers
of petty and mindless laws have been enacted to ensure
the viability of the system. In 1964, as La Guma observes, "over 20 percent of the non-white population had
spent some days in prison for one crime or another" (3).

When the prisoner Morgan is informed by his cell mate Gus
that Adams has been imprisoned "for talking against the
govvernmen," Morgan puts into perspective the high
statistic of crime that is attributed to nonwhites:

> "Talking against the govvernmen," Morgan mused.   "A
> man go to jail for almost anything nowadays, hey.
> Talking against the govvernmen.   I'd like to do some
> talking against the ―――― govvernmen.   Ja, a man go
> to jail for all kinds of things."   [p. 101]

Hence, the prison comprises "ragged street-corner hood-
lums, shivering drunks, thugs in cheap flamboyant clothes
and knowledgeable looks, murderers, robbers, housebreak-
ers, petty criminals, rapists, loiterers and simple
permit-offenders . . ." [p. 19].   And their faces are
described as follows:

> All around him [George] was a composition of faces,
> old faces, young faces, middle-aged faces; faces
> burned with stubble or cicatriced with scars; bloated
> faces and depraved faces; vicious faces and kind
> faces; faces hopeless, impersonal, happy, frightened,
> brutal.   It was as if all the experiences of mankind
> had been thrust into these few cubic yards of steel-
> confined space.   [p. 16]

The prison is a "stone country" where guards and
prisoners are "the enforced inhabitants of another
country, another world."   It is "a world without beauty;
a lunar barrenness of stone and steel and locked doors."
In the prison "no trees" grow "and the only shade [is]
found in the shadow" of the prison's "cliffs of walls."
In the summer the prison broils and in the winter it chat-
ters; the only music permitted is "composed out of the
slip-slap of bare feet, the grinding of boots, counter-
pointed by shouted orders, the slam of doors and the
tintinnabulation of heavy keys" [p. 18].   The prison is
the last line of defense of the racist system.   It is a
place where the indignant and the malicious of the
disadvantaged nonwhite population are held in and barri-
caded from the secure and comfortable white population
[p. 81].
    Like the country of which the prison is an extension,
the prison is divided into three rigid sections to house
the white, colored, and black population.   Although

George Adams and Jefferson belong to the same "illegal"
political organization and have been arrested together
for the same "illegal" act, inside the prison they are
divided by race. Hence, when Adams asks Jefferson if
they will in fact be held together, he is told: "No.
Sorry. This jail is a small something of what they want
to make the country. Everybody separate, boy: White,
African, Coloured. Regulations for everybody, and a
white boss with a gun and a stick" [p. 20]. Not only are
the prisoners segregated by "high grilles" but the food
and general treatment of the races are different. At
breakfast time "plain corn mush" is served to the nonwhite prisoners while their counterparts in the white
section receive "mush with milk and sugar and slices of
bread" [p. 50]. Whereas the nonwhite prisoners endure a
rigid regime of work and brutality on the part of the
white prison guards, the white prisoners are permitted to
spend time outside their cells and to engage in exercise
and other forms of recreation.

Inside the "warren of cells, cages, corridors and
yards" of the prison, "built in Victorian times," the
guards do not follow any of the regulations that have
been established for the governing of the prison; nor do
they respect any of the rights to which prisoners are
entitled. When Adams insists that it is his "right to
have blankets," Yusef the Turk replies: "Rights. You
reckon you got rights, man? Listen, mate, only these
—— warders got rights. They tell you what is rights"
[p. 51].

The prison is the stone country where guards and
prisoners are forced to be together, and because of the
power invested in the guards by the state, they are able
to wield their authority in whichever way they choose.
The guards put great stress on keeping "everything under
control" and are prepared to wield brutal authority to
ensure this control. The control takes many forms,
including denial of bare necessities such as blankets,
refusal of meals, detention in the Isolation Block and
the fearsome Hole, and the design of a system where the
most brutal prisoners are permitted to mete out cruel
punishment on those who show contempt for, defy, and
disobey the guards' authority. In an extended metaphor
where the prison cat stalks a mouse, La Guma indicates
the relative positions of the guards and the prisoners:
"The mouse, small and grey, had no intention of being
devoured, but there, in the hot glare of the sun that

practically blinded it, and dizzy from the blows it had
received from the cat's great paw, there seemed little
hope." When the mouse "suddenly . . . attempt[s] a dash
sideways," the cat "club[s] it casually," an action that
receives the "chuckling" approval of the guards: "The
three guards were watching, with fascination, the punishment of the mouse, chuckling, as if they felt a natural
association with the feline sadism" [p. 124]. Behind the
"grille," however, "a crowd of prisoners" associating
themselves with the plight of the mouse, "also watched."
The cat watches its victim squirm and from time to time a
"clubbed paw reache[s] out and nudge[s] " the mouse. This
causes tremendous pain to the mouse and it remains
"balled up." But the mouse is not ready to give up the
fight; it continues "waiting with tiny, beating heart for
another chance to escape the doom that waited for it with
horrid patience." And when the overconfident cat makes
the mistake of rising "up on all fours," the mouse
streaks "straight forward under the long belly and out
past the swishing tail" [p. 126]. For this yeoman effort
the mouse is congratulated by the prisoners with "a vast
roaring sound in its ears." Disappointed that the cat
has failed to hold its victim, one of the guards tries
unsuccessfully to block the passage of the mouse. As the
cat continues to pursue the mouse, the mouse dashes for
the "dark hole of a drain-pipe" and enters it a second or
two before the cat's sabered paw can slash at it. The
success of the "pain-wracked" mouse now causes the
prisoners to chuckle "over the disappointment of the cat
as it crouched waiting at the hole" [pp. 126-27].

The "clubbing" of the prisoners by the guards begins
as soon as the prisoner enters the dilapidated building.
Should any prisoners arrive at an inopportune time, as in
the case of Adams, they are denied basic facilities of
the prison such as blankets, eating utensils, and a much-
needed bath. In response to the prisoners having a bath,
one of the guards replies: "Jussus, man, I am not going
to wait. Going off now, jong. These bastards can wash
in the morning, to hell with it. I'm not working blerry
overtime" [p. 27]. The contempt that the guards have for
the prisoners is displayed openly the very moment that
the prisoners report to the "Reception Hall" to be finger-
printed and classified. Whereas the guards take the
liberty to insult the various prisoners, the prisoners on
the other hand must show obedience and cowed respect.
Hence, derogatory remarks such as "Come on, you ——

kaffir. Do you think this is a ---- location?" or "What
kind of a blerry name is that? Christ, you look like a
---- parrot" or "Shut your ---- mouths, you bliksems.
You reckon this is a ---- circus?" abound [p. 19]. The
"political prisoners" are disliked in particular because
they represent a threat to the continuance of the guards
and the racist regime's authority [p. 24].

Contempt and insult are but two minor forms of psychological oppression in the prison. To ensure control of
and "harmony" in the prison, the guards create disunity
among the prisoners by choosing a few brutal ringleaders
to keep the defiant and troublesome prisoners in tow.
The reward for such services is mild and privileged treatment. This is demonstrated in the case of George Adams,
who believes firmly that one must challenge what is wrong
in the system. Because of this belief he joined a political organization and carried out protest action against
the regime. He is arrested for his belief and now finds
himself in prison. But Adams continues his crusade for
justice inside the prison and thus runs headlong into
opposition from the guards. The most hated guard is named
Fatso. Fatso cannot accept "talking back" from any
prisoner and thus he takes an instant dislike to Adams,
who in requesting his legitimate share of prison blankets
and mat displays a nonchalant air of disrespect for
Fatso. Fatso now turns to Butcherboy, the brutal prison
bully, to punish the defiant one [pp. 62-63]. Hence
Butcherboy accosts Adams at the first opportunity; but
Adams persists in his defiance and questions the efficiency of the prison: "Well, why don't they run this jail
proper?" [p. 75]. The remark causes Fatso's face to
"writhe like a puddle of boiling lava" and he is reminded
that Adams is "one of those slim men, hey? A clever
darky." Fatso senses rare defeat when the store boy
issues Adams "a spare mug" and when the other prisoners
disbelievingly stare at him, he fumes with rage. Fatso
realizes his defeat and this rankles him. It is now left
to Fatso's henchman, Butcherboy, to take the necessary
revenge [p. 76].

Defiance of the prison guards is a rare happening.
Most of the prisoners accept the prison system as it
exists and thus ensure the perpetuation of the unjust
situation. George Adams naively imagines that because an
unjust socioeconomic and political system has sent all
the nonwhite prisoners to the prison, the inmates are in
fact comrades and, therefore, work together: "'Well,

we're all in here together, man,' George Adams told him.
'Might as well share the work.'" But Yusef the Turk
informs Adams that the prison is a veritable jungle where
the strong brutalize the weak and where the intelligent
prisoners "learn to catch wire" so as to "have an easy
time in this blerry place" [p. 51]. Such a pecking-order
assures and protects disunity among the prisoners and
ensures an unchallenged prison system. The prison is
very much a place where everyone takes care of himself.
It is a world where the Casbah Kid, alias Albert March,
and Butcherboy Williams are at home. The Casbah Kid and
Butcherboy are marvelous creations of both the observed
reality and the transformation that occur in the creative
mind.

The Casbah Kid is nineteen years old and is awaiting
trial for murdering a drunken man who had refused to
surrender his watch to him. La Guma observes that "the
Casbah Kid actually spent time with me in the same prison
cell and I had a chance to observe him" (4). Adams's
role as psychiatrist is important to understand the
Casbah Kid. La Guma recalls that the young murderer was
"taciturn, unrepentant, and willing to accept the punishment meted out to him" (5). Since this attitude of the
Casbah Kid impressed the writer very much, because in a
way it contains the elements of responsibility and defiance that are so often sought in La Guma's characters, a
special effort was made to understand the motives behind
his actions. Beginning as an uncommunicative and heartless person, Adams slowly, through human kindness and
concern, leads the Casbah Kid to accept, begrudgingly, a
view of man and the world that is less desperate and hopeless than before. His departure from the prison at the
end of the novel "is exactly how it happened in reality"
(6). The Casbah Kid does not believe in the reward or
retribution system of heaven and hell; for him everything
has been predesigned and he accepts his impending fate
without concern. He believes that "you can't change
things, mos," and considers those who want to do so to
be "crack" [p. 14].

The Casbah Kid does not trust anyone, nor does he care
for the welfare of others. When he and Adams are
together in the Isolation Block and Adams is asked for
tobacco by Gus, the prisoner who occupies the adjoining
cell, the Casbah Kid responds contemptuously: "Blerry
bum-slingers. . . . Always bumming. No twak, no this,
no that." Adams concludes then: "You poor sod, you

poor, poor sod, you going to die and you don't give a
damn about yourself and about anybody else . . ." [p.
92]. The Casbah Kid is a loner who harbors deep thoughts
of revenge. When he is unfairly and brutally beaten by
Butcherboy, the reader is told that "vengeance slipped
into his mind with the ease of the sprockets of an oiled
wheel into the links of a greased chain" [p. 35].

While the prisoners are embroiled in their own energy-
sapping and violent disputes, the prison system of "stone
and iron" stands unchallenged and the guardians of this
system encourage the dissension among the prisoners. The
most celebrated case in the novel is that of Butcherboy
Williams and his fight with Yusef the Turk. In the story
"Tattoo Marks and Nails," a slight version of the
Butcherboy appears; and in "Out of Darkness" the mildly
deranged Ou Kakkelak refers to Butcherboy as "an ape-man
roaming a jungle" and contends that in the cave of the
prison "the cave man is king." According to La Guma,
"every prison in South Africa has a Butcherboy and any
portrait of prison life must inevitably include a description of such a character" (8). There are few instances
in La Guma's writing when he describes a character in the
severe manner that he does Butcherboy. He is described
throughout the novel in animalistic terms. His torso is
referred to as "ape-like" and it is "covered with tattooed decorations: hands holding hands, a skull-and-
crossbones, a Union Jack, a dripping dagger, and various
other emblems consistent with his barbarism" [p. 31]. He
has a "neolithic head," "a fist like a mallet," and when
he is asleep his "heavy form stir[s] with the effort of
his brontosaurian snores" [pp. 32, 36]. He has "blood-
flecked, gorilla eyes," "mossy teeth like desecrated
tombstones," and "harsh, carious breath" that reminds
Adams "of overturned dustbins in the grime-slippery
lobbies of mouldering tenements and the smell of latrine
buckets in hot cells" [p. 65]. To keep the allegiance of
his brutal and "obsequious retinue," Brakes Peterson,
Pinks, Moos, and Squinteye Samuels, and to demonstrate
both to the other prisoners and to the guards who use him
deliberately to keep brutal order among the prisoners
that he is the most powerful prisoner, Butcherboy
addresses and treats other prisoners in a harsh manner.
When "a sudden uproar from another part of the cell"
interrupts his talk with Solly, he bellows: "Shut your
——ing mouths, you sonamabitches." When he walks
through the cell he kicks "his way through the tangle of

bodies" [pp. 32, 33]. His power is such that all new-
comers to the prison have to be seen and scrutinized by
him. In the cases of an identified prisoner who refuses
to "jump" to his call and the Casbah Kid, who respects no
authority, Butcherboy uses his mallet fists and his ape-
like torso to pummel them into pulp and hated submission.

George Adams, however, is as little prepared to accept
Butcherboy's brutal authority as he is to accept the
authority of the hated regime that has placed him in
prison. Adams sees Butcherboy's brutal bullying as being
in the same class as that of the bullying of the authorities both inside and outside the prison. In such a world
of brute force, color is of no consequence. Adams knows
that Butcherboy cares about his kinglike status only, and
that to ensure that status he is ready to cooperate with
the racist authorities at the expense of the other prisoners. When Butcherboy considers it his duty to punish
Adams so as to uphold the wounded authority of Fatso, the
small but defiant Adams refuses to cower. This display
of defiance infuriates Butcherboy and he promises to
"break your ——ing neck." Adams, however, contemplates
kicking Butcherboy "in the balls and hope for the best"
[p. 66]. It is at this juncture that Yusef the Turk
intervenes on Adams's behalf and a fight is arranged
between Yusef and Butcherboy. The fight is described in
graphic and gory detail and it ends only when an
exhausted Butcherboy "stumble[s] away" into "the middle
of his silent knot of henchmen and satellites" where the
Casbah Kid unobtrusively stabs him to death [p. 88].
Although Adams's natural bent toward compassion makes him
feel sorry for Butcherboy, he is unsentimental enough to
believe that even in such a corrupt sociopolitical
climate as South Africa, Butcherboy carries with him a
human responsibility that must challenge the racist
society's brutality. Otherwise, he is a willing ghost of
the night who accepts his brutal and stultifying role and
his death, therefore, comes as a relief and a blessing to
the other prisoners.

A further form of brutal punishment that the powerful
prisoners engage in is the so-called "trial." The trial
comprised a "mock court" where the most depraved inmate
would brutalize a rebellious or offending prisoner.
Butcherboy desires such a trial in the case of Yusef the
Turk, but Yusef and the cellmates who witness the subsequent "fair fight" refuse to concede to his demand. In
discussing the trial La Guma gives the reader a further

insight into the brutality of prison life.

The mark of all La Guma's writing is found in his belief that no matter how oppressive a situation may be there is always some room for challenging oppression and bringing about change. As indicated earlier, the character George Adams resembles La Guma in some ways. His role in the story is not that of being the hero, but rather, as La Guma indicates, "he is a telescope through which to see what is going around" (9). Adams, however, becomes more than a telescope; he assumes again the role of being the recorder of events but, since he is an experienced man of the political world, he also attempts to teach the lessons he has learned. Both Adams and La Guma are members of an "illegal" political organization when they are arrested. Both believe that the oppressive racist system of South Africa can be changed through the oppressed uniting and mounting concerted political action. Both are aware of the rights a human being should enjoy whether inside the stone country of socio-economic and political oppression of the general South African system or inside the brutal stone country of South Africa's prisons. George Adams and Alex La Guma are therefore placed in the roles of defying oppression wherever it rears its ugly head in South Africa. La Guma projects himself well in the character: the reader is left with a concerned, compassionate narrator who does not intrude too much in the action as it occurs.

The spirit of organized defiance that Adams shows outside the prison is brought into the prison by him. By observing Adams's maneuvers the reader is given some insight into why opposition has generally failed in the prison. One of the first discouraging observations that Adams makes is that in the "half-world" of prison there is "an atmosphere of every-man-for-himself." Since Adams grew up in the slums he recognizes at once that in the prison are to be found "the treacherous and the wily, the cringers and the boot-lickers, the violent and the domineering, the smooth-talkers and the savage, the bewildered and the helpless." Here in the prison "the strong preyed on the weak, and the strong and brutal acknowledged a sort of nebulous alliance among themselves for the terrorisation of the underlings" [p. 37]. The prisoners are preoccupied with how to survive and how to have an easy existence. Hence, as Yusef the Turk points out to Adams, many prisoners injure themselves deliberately or seek fights with the guards simply "to get a little

easier treatment" [p. 70]. Generally, because of the
brutal regime existing in the prison, the prisoners
accept their deprived situation and, like the indicated
position of the oppressed outside the prison, they leave
their trust in God, sing hymns, and attend the Sunday
church service in the prison.

Unaware of the general lethargic malaise and pecking-
order of the prisoners and buoyed by his own belief that
"you did what you decided was the right thing, and then
accepted the consequences," Adams sets out to oppose the
injustice of the prison system and to unite the inmates
so as to take common and concerted action against their
oppressors. To this end, he even dreams that the violent
energy of Butcherboy can be used in political work.
Adams recognizes, however, the "divide and rule" policy
of the prison authorities and sadly reflects: "What a
waste; here they got us fighting each other like dogs."
But he is not completely daunted by the status quo and is
ready to recommend to the prisoners that they "strike for
better diet, mos" [p. 74].

Adams's thinking, however, does not obtain any
adherents and he is unable to prevent the brutal fight
between Butcherboy and Yusef the Turk that leads to
Butcherboy's death. He does not lose his compassion:
Adams distributes his food rations and cigarettes freely
among those who are without. Even though he is the butt
of Butcherboy's violence, Adams admits in a bewildering
way to the Casbah Kid that he is "kind of sorry for that
poor basket, Butcherboy" [p. 90]. Adams's compassion, of
course, stems from the fact that he is aware that the
prisoners are blind and unthinking victims of a vicious
system that desires to reduce both the oppressed outside
and inside the prison to the violence and lack of compassion of the stone and iron society the regime has built.
The only success that Adams has is in helping the Casbah
Kid to unload the emotional and psychological burden he
is carrying and to make him aware that there are people
in the world who care for him. But, as in the outside
world, he is unable to persuade others to see the injustice of their situation and to organize against it.

The escape, one that actually occurred while La Guma
was in prison, that Gus, Morgan, and Koppe are involved
in must be seen not simply as a routine occurrence at a
prison. It is a deliberately chosen outlet to escape the
prison's brutality but also to demonstrate defiance
against the unjust system. To confirm the fact that the

prisoners consider escaping from the prison as an act of
defiance, the reader is shown the reaction of the other
prisoners to Gus, Morgan, and Koppe's escape:

> It was an uproar caused by hundreds of shouting, chant-
> ing voices punctuated with the clamour of hundreds of
> metal mugs being banged against iron doors and stone
> walls in an irregular, cacophonic chorus. The prison-
> ers were jeering the warders, singing, and cheering on
> the escapees. [p. 156]

The cat and mouse symbolism is especially appropriate
here. Although brutalized on a daily basis by the "cats"
(the guards), the "mice" (the prisoners) are always trying to escape the clutches of the guards. And as in the
earlier case, the prison audience hopes and cheers when
the three prisoners try to escape. Until now George
Adams has had little to cheer about, being always aware
of his own inability to unite the prisoners behind the
purpose of challenging the unjust system. In the escape
of Gus, Morgan, and Koppe, Adams finally recognizes "the
solidarity of the underworld" [p. 156]. But his excite-
ment turns to disappointment and frustration when Gus and
Morgan are captured: "They got them. Those ―― guards
got them" [p. 157].

It is La Guma's firm belief that all the participants
both outside and inside the prison are victims of a
racist system that reduces South Africa to a heartless
land of stone and iron. Although his work is singularly
concerned with showing that the social environment causes
the disastrous behavior of the oppressed of South Africa,
he is, however, not a propagandist who hammers away at
political messages to make his point. Hence, in The
Stone Country, he alludes only to the question of
whether the prison creates the violent conditions that
exist there or whether the violence is brought into the
prison from outside. The white judge who sentences the
Casbah Kid to death for stabbing another man refuses to
admit that the racist system of South Africa has caused
the emergence of types such as the Casbah Kid. His
belief is that the "state and local authorities" have
undertaken "immense expenditure" to improve "social conditions" and he rejects the plea that the Casbah Kid is an
unfortunate and unwilling product of "a class" and "surroundings where violence and drunkenness are an everyday
occurrence" [p. 166]. To the judge it is the Casbah Kid

who brings violence into the prison. Morgan's story of
"the Prophet Daniel [and] the king of Egyp' or Baby-lon"
differs somewhat from the judge and the guards' view of
the situation. Morgan notes that the regime and the
guards believe that the prisoners bring their brutality
with them when they arrive in the jail: "You know, Gus,
. . . these Dutchmen always telling you you bring these
things in with you? Is never in the blerry jail when you
arrive. No, you bring it in with you." Then he tells
the story of how Daniel stayed the whole night in the
lions' den and "the lions don't touch him a bogger." The
king's amazement at Daniel being alive is reported by
Morgan as follows:

> "Morning, Daniel," the king, he say to ou Daniel.
> "How did you spend the night, hey?" And ou Daniel,
> he say, "Not too bad, King. But these lions, they was
> a little troublesome."
>   Well the King, he's just like this: "I's sorry to
> hear that, Daniel, but you must have brought them with
> you." [p. 130]

La Guma's view is that the prisoners are victims of an
external society where lions roam freely about. When
they are wounded to some extent by these lions they are
thrown into a den inside the prison where more lions
roam. In this sense there is no escape from the lion's
den, because South Africa both outside and inside the
prison is the stone country and it is also a veritable
jungle where the powerful dominate the weak. Adams
learns this lesson in jail and he is left with a deep
sense of frustration. He knows that only when the
oppressed are fully aware of their predicament and are
prepared to work together to overthrow the yoke of the
oppressor, as in the case of his dream [pp. 112-13], will
they be able to destroy the country of stone that has
until now made them prey to the lions in the den.

Chapter Six
Awareness and Defiance:
In the Fog of the Season's End

In the Fog of the Season's End is Alex La Guma's fourth
long work. It was published in 1972 in London by Heinemann, and although it appeared six years after La Guma
had left South Africa it had been conceived and substan-
tially written while he was still there (1). The novel
is dedicated to the memory of Basil February, a close
personal and political friend of La Guma's who decided to
continue the struggle against the racist regime of South
Africa from outside the South African borders as a guerrilla activist. In 1967, while involved in a raid,
February and other guerrilla activists were killed in
Zambia. Once more, the dedication indicates clearly that
the purpose of writing the novel is to demonstrate the
rapid development of both passive and military active
opposition to the racist regime of South Africa. The
author chooses two chief characters and a large supporting cast to show how the oppressive policies of the
South African regime finally led oppressed South Africans
to a position of defiance and revolution. Through the
underground organizers Tekwane and Beukes and through the
brutal organization of the South African police, the
reader is prepared for the impending and inevitable warlike situation between oppressor and oppressed that
Beukes predicts at the end of the novel. As Isaac and
the other two guerrilla activists leave South Africa for
military training outside the country, Beukes defiantly
and triumphantly states:

> . . . they have gone to war in the name of a suffering
> people. What the enemy himself has created, these
> will become battle-grounds, and what we see now is
> only the tip of an iceberg of resentment against an
> ignoble regime, the tortured victims of hatred and
> humiliation. And those who persist in hatred and
> humiliation must prepare. Let them prepare hard and
> fast--they do not have long to wait. (2)

In this sense they are following in the valiant and
heroic footsteps of those warriors, such as the Bushmen,
who "were first to fight" the oppressors. And since
Isaac at the end of the novel is to become the guerrilla
activist Paul, his presence near the "ochre figures" in
the museum is symbolic of his warrior status [p. 14].

All of La Guma's works that have been discussed to
this point have dealt with the injustice of the apartheid
system and its brutalizing effects on both the oppressed
and the oppressor. And in every book La Guma has
attempted to create conditions of defiance through which
the South African people can be liberated from a system
that has reduced them to unfeeling, heartless beings. In
the early books, however, the attempt at reform peters
out because of the inability of the reformers to circum-
vent successfully the immense power of the South African
police. In In the Fog of the Season's End, La Guma
still portrays the power of the police, but he now shows
that with constant work and determination it is possible
to challenge and to defeat the "ignoble" system. In
response to the observation that the novel differs somewhat from other South African writers' offerings on
apartheid in that it does not merely lament the system of
injustice in South Africa but actually applauds a positive program of action that will lead to armed conflict
between the oppressed and the oppressor, La Guma says the
following:

> Well, you are quite right in saying that the novel
> presents an attitude that we have now protested enough
> and that we should now fight. Well, I believe that I
> had earlier set down to a certain extent anyway the
> protest against the situation in our country. All of
> us have bewailed this situation and others will con-
> tinue to do so. But, as I say, trying to convey a
> picture of South Africa one must also realize that
> apart from people bewailing their fate, there are also
> people struggling against it, and that the political
> and revolutionary movement in South Africa was a part
> of the South African scene and that one way or another
> people have always been fighting against this situa-
> tion. The political and revolutionary movement has to
> appear somewhere in the picture and I hope In the Fog
> of the Season's End is a start. I tried to present
> the underground struggle against the regime as part of
> the picture of South Africa. (3)

La Guma confirms this hope further by citing the Guinean writer Conte Saigon Tidiany, whose M̲a̲r̲t̲y̲r̲s̲ defiantly and triumphantly proclaims that the centuries of enslavement that Africans have suffered at the hands of their European colonial oppressors "Will be shattered like the spider web / In the fog of the season's end" (4).

The emphasis of I̲n̲ ̲t̲h̲e̲ ̲F̲o̲g̲ ̲o̲f̲ ̲t̲h̲e̲ ̲S̲e̲a̲s̲o̲n̲'̲s̲ ̲E̲n̲d̲ is on the positive and revolutionary development of the South African resistance and liberation movement (5). But to appreciate the new and defiant response to some of the oppressed, La Guma once more has to return to the theme of his earlier work to show how the protest arose. Hence the novel returns to the familiar theme of the devastating and tragic effects that the socioeconomic and political situation has on the oppressed people. Once again the reader is taken on a slow and painful tour through the human destruction that the apartheid regime and its system have contrived. In the first chapter of the novel, La Guma shows us the now familiar side of apartheid. The municipal park that Beukes is resting in segregates the benches between "Whites" and "Non-Whites." Behind the "maze of pathways" leading to the museum is an "open-air restaurant" reserved for "Whites Only" [p. 8]. A sign near the top of the statue of Rhodes points toward "the segregated lavatories" [p. 12]. The museum that Beukes finally enters once had separate "Whites" and "Non-Whites" entrances but now begrudgingly permits non-white visitors on specially set aside days [p. 18]. It is in the park facing the museum that Beukes confronts Beatie Adams and observes the inferior manner in which whites treat their nonwhite "nannys" [p. 11]. Although Beatie is pushing a pram that contains a white child she is not permitted to sit on the "green benches" that have been reserved for "Whites Only" [p. 9].

The beaches of South Africa are divided along racial lines, with the inferior pieces being set aside for the nonwhites. Bennett's failure to house Beukes is compounded by his boast that they "had a helluva time at the beach." This boast forces Beukes to think bitterly of Bennet having pleasure at the "coloured beach" [p. 19]. Discrimination exists at the railway station as well. Apart from the separate racial entrances to the station and the different compartments and seats for the races, nonwhites are also forbidden to cross the "White foot-bridge." When Beukes circumvents the security-police network he considers the use of the footbridge, but he is

deterred by the forceful reminder that "a Coloured man
had recently been sentenced to twenty pounds or ten days"
for using the "White bridge." The magistrate had further
warned the fined person that "sterner measures would be
taken if the practice continued . . ." [p. 64]. And, as
Beukes discovers at the age of seven, the schools as well
are divided rigidly along color lines: "They had been
told that they would be giving a special performance of
their concert for a White school. That was really the
first time that the little boy had realized that children
called 'White' attended separate schools" [pp. 83-84].

Perhaps the most serious indignity and injustice the
apartheid system perpetrates is to force all blacks over
the age of sixteen years to carry the hated pass book.
In In the Fog of the Season's End, La Guma gives this
aspect of the racist system much attention. In what
occurs a countless number of times every day in South
Africa La Guma makes the reader vividly aware of the total power that the regime wields over the oppressed [p.
80]. La Guma goes on to depict a discussion between a
brutal, contemptuous white South African policeman and a
black man, who, although his credentials are impeccable,
is subjected to the terrifying situation of apartheid
South Africa. The black man is humiliated by the officer's use of the derogatory denotation of "kaffir," by
his insolent and absurd questioning, by his contempt and
brutality, and by the laws of the country that subject a
citizen to so much indignity. Without the pass the black
man is not permitted to live in his township, to travel
from one place to another, to work, and, in fact, to
exist, as indicated by the policeman. But even with the
pass the black man is not permitted to have his family
visit or live with him without prior permission or he
stands to have "the wrath of the Devil and all his
minions" [p. 81] invoked against him. The policeman also
reminds the man that he is "not allowed to leave" his job
with his present employer without permission, nor can he
leave his present place of abode for another without
consent.

It is the humiliation that Elias Tekwane suffers at
the pass office that spurs him on to revolt against the
racist system. It is in the pass office where he is made
aware that without a pass the authorities can prevent a
man from attending the funeral of a brother [p. 124].
Tekwane is informed by the black clerk who aids the
white commissioner that obtaining his pass is finally the

moment when he "will become part of what the White people
have done for this land. The big bosses have ordained
that only when you carry the pass will you be a man" [p.
125]. One of the most humiliating aspects related to the
obtaining of his pass is when Tekwane's age is disputed
by the black clerk. The clerk refuses to accept that
Tekwane "with a beard and all" can be seventeen years
only. After being accused of being "'a skelm, a cheat'"
and a liar [p. 126], Tekwane is forced to remove his
pants so that his "true" age can be determined. The
sighting of his genitals leads to a new round of insult
and humiliation on the part of the pass officers. But no
matter how much Tekwane protests he is declared to be
"'twenty, and twenty years you are'" [p. 127].

Since the pass is the most hated symbol of the black
man's oppression, it has often been used to stir up mass
resistance against the South African regime. In In the
Fog of the Season's End, La Guma refers to the celebrated 1960 Sharpeville uprising against the regime. On
that occasion, as noted by the sergeant at the police
station, rumors were that the "whole black population of
the country had been called on to defy the country's laws
. . ." [p. 99]. While the sergeant was plagued by rumor
in the township "the word had gone round for the surrender or destruction of all passes that day" [p. 101]. In
keeping with the regime's "no compromise, no discussion"
policy, hundreds of police and soldiers were rushed to
the scene armed in the most terrifying and warlike way.
At "about two in the afternoon . . . the mechanisms of
Sten-submachine guns and revolvers clacked and clicked
with sounds of metallic efficiency" [p 103]. This display of power spurred the "fists clutching" protesters on
to greater chants of "Take the passes, we don't want the
passes." Then, as La Guma notes, "for some reason or
another, a policeman shot into the noise" and the people
began to scatter in fear and panic. Further volleys of
firepower led to the destruction of many of the protesters [p. 104]. The horror of what occurred at Sharpeville stirred many of the oppressed into greater
militancy against the regime and led inevitably to the
decision to reinforce passive demonstration with underground armed conflict. This action stirred Tekwane,
Beukes, and the other active protesters of the South
African system to take on the many sacrifices and risks
that La Guma details in the novel.

A further cruel irritant of the apartheid system is

the enforcement of the Group Areas Act. The act ensures
that where the races must share common territory this
territory be rigidly divided by race and that where
possible the races do not have any contact. Hence,
throughout South Africa, and especially in the populated
urban center, residential areas and townships are set
aside for the various groups. And as is everywhere
common under apartheid, the best areas are reserved for
the white community. When faced with a situation as
depicted in In the Fog of the Season's End where a nonwhite suburb is situated next to a white one, the regime,
with little concern for the historical, cultural, and
socioeconomic aspects of the community, simply uproots
the community and deposits the inhabitants in deserted,
sewage- and electricity-less townships. In place of the
nonwhite community a new white suburb is constructed.
Beukes passes through such an area and observes that
"whole blocks had disappeared, leaving empty, flattened
lots surrounded by battered survivors" [p. 26]. With the
community gone it seems to Beukes as if they "were in the
main street of a ghost town" with telltale signs of a
once-vibrant communal life having been reduced to destruction and tragedy [pp. 26-27]. The inhabitants now find
themselves in a new township where the government-built
houses have walls that peel "like diseased skin" and the
sad children stare "out over fences like shabby glove-
puppets" [p. 164]. Unable to take their frustration out
on those who oppress them the township dwellers turn
their violence on each other and make an already devastating place more tragic and brutal.

Apartheid takes its toll in the workplace as well.
Here it runs the whole gamut from simple disrespect and
contempt for black workers to serious exploitation of
their labor. The case of Beatie, the colored nanny, has
already been referred to. In Tekwane's situation,
although he slaves for long hours at Wasserman's store,
he is offered the meager wage of "three shillings and
sixpence every Friday" and is fed "left-overs" [p. 76].
His job at Wasserman's is ensured while he accepts his
lowly status and poor pay, but when he dares to relate to
Wasserman his failure to be accepted as a volunteer
soldier, he is greeted with racial hatred for daring to
"interest [himself] in the business of White people." He
is then commanded to "clear off" and not to be seen
around "again" [p. 79].

At Isaac's workplace the nonwhite workers are dis-

missed as "boys" and they are employed as messengers and
"tea boys." Isaac works for an American petroleum
company that displays very boldly in the foyer of the
reception office an "Arabian king." But, as Isaac notes,
"for all the oil he owned, he was still a darkie in this
country" and would be treated so by the "beautifully
preserved" white typists of the "Master Race." The
"boys" were noticed by the whites only "when an order had
to be given or when a favour was required, otherwise they
were part of the furniture, like the grey typewriter
covers, the coat rack, the tiny bottles of liquid eraser,
copies of memos" [p. 111].

The fate of the black worker is irrelevant to the
white community:

> Black people came into the White-proclaimed city each
> morning to do the menial work and left each evening to
> return to the Locations, the Townships, set aside for
> them like ghettoes. They did not belong with the
> midday restaurants, the hotels, the apartment houses,
> the landscaped gardens and the sundrenched beaches on
> Saturday afternoons, tea on a terrace or cocktails in
> a plastic and chrome lounge. [p. 112]

For the chief clerk of the fuel-oil department the "boys"
symbolize the servants at the "company's annual outing to
the Country Club." They are the waiters who will serve
"cokes and sandwiches and [wash] up glasses" for "ten
shillings for the day" [pp. 112-13].

Migrant labor is even more devastating as a discrimina-
tory labor practice. The industrial development of South
Africa is based on cheap black labor. For the important,
sensitive industries such as the gold mines the industri-
alists search for docile black laborers from neighboring
countries and the rural areas. These workers are sifted
and graded like slabs of meat and they are then transported like sheep and cows to their workplace. They are
contracted for periods of time, housed in compounds, not
permitted to have a family life, and generally treated as
company slaves. And when a worker is taken ill, as in
the case of the miner that Tekwane sees, he is simply
allowed to go home and die without financial compensation. Tekwane's father had been one of the miners who
instead of coming home to die ignobly and poverty-
stricken of pthisis had died in a mine accident. As
compensation for his life, his family received "forty

pounds" while "the widows of white miners killed along-
side [Tekwane's father] had been awarded fifteen pounds a
month for the rest of their lives" [p. 74].

There is no legally recognized procedure in the South
African labor system to redress the injustices that are
perpetrated against the black workers. Black unions are
not recognized and to strike against an employer is an
illegal act. Yet, strikes are carried out regularly, as
in the case of the laundry workers whom Tekwane assists.
Africans are, according to the law, "not workers, but
servants, and the contract bound them fast." Hence, whenever a strike occurs, the management usually summons the
police, who break up the strikes by using "truncheons" on
the strikers [p. 133].

La Guma believes strongly that apartheid cannot
survive without the brutal enforcement of the South
African police. He agrees entirely with the "heavy
letters" on the blank wall facing the harbor that once
you set your feet ashore on South African soil "You Are
Now Entering The Police State" [p. 24]. La Guma explains
that in South Africa "we [literally] live with the
police. Black people are continually being harassed by
the police. If it is not from the Pass laws among the
African people it is for drunkenness or other social problems among other communities" (6). La Guma goes on to
say that "the presence of the police" in his work is not
only intentional, but "inevitable" (7). In particular
the security police are singled out because in his own
political life in South Africa La Guma was their constant
victim. This personal experience permits La Guma to
provide the reader with intimate and authentic portrayals
of the police and their nefarious work. The description
of the police who arrest, interrogate, and brutalize
Tekwane is a masterpiece of observation and authentic
commentary. The major at the police station is described
as follows:

> He was broad and seemed to be constructed of a series
> of pink ovals: balding head and fat oval face, fat
> neck that topped curving shoulders which formed the
> upper curve of the big oval that was his rotund trunk:
> he could have been an advertisement for good cheer.
> He was in shirtsleeves, and the hands which emerged
> from the starched cuffs were pink and plump and oval.
> Only his eyes were small and round and shiny, like two
> glass beads; small, bright, conscienceless eyes. Yet

when he spoke his voice took on a friendly, sympathet-
ic tone, like a doctor advising a patient. [p. 3]

The level of education and intelligence of the South
African police is generally low, with the emphasis in
hiring being placed on blind loyalty to the apartheid
system and to brutality. Since, however, the security
police have to face the better educated and more sophisti-
cated members of the resistance movement, the upper
echelon of the police has attracted men of better intelligence who employ reason and intimidation in equal
amounts. The major belongs to the latter group, and his
method of dealing with Tekwane differs somewhat from that
of the other two policemen who arrested Tekwane. The
major begins his interrogation by lamenting the fact that
the oppressed people are so ungrateful of "what we, our
Government, have done for your people." He goes on to
argue as follows:

We have given you nice jobs, houses, education.
Education, ja. Take Education for instance. We
have allowed you people to get education, your own
special schools, but you are not satisfied. No, you
want more than what you get. I have heard that some
of your young people even want to learn mathematics.
What good is mathematics to you? You see, you people
are not the same as we are. We can understand these
things, mathematics. We know the things which are
best for you. Yet you want to be like the Whites.
It's impossible. You want this country to be like
Ghana, the Congo. Look what they did in the Congo.
You people will never be able to govern anything. But
we understand that you must have certain things,
rights, so we have arranged for you to have the things
you need, under our supervision. [p. 4]

The major claims that it is his duty to save the blacks
from dissatisfied people such as Tekwane, who, he claims,
has been "misled by certain other people—clever people,
priests, lawyers, Communists" [p. 4]. He sees it as his
task to "stop" Tekwane, "to destroy your organization"
[p. 5]. Although the major encourages Tekwane to speak
his mind, he also indicates clearly to him that should
Tekwane fail to provide the names and details of his
resistance movement he will not hesitate to punish him.
    The major's promise to Tekwane proves hollow, because

as soon as Tekwane informs him that he will not cooperate
in the interrogation, the major threatens to have his
"balls out." And this, of course, as the Prologue shows,
is the level on which the South African police function
best. The methods that the South African police employ
to preserve and to enforce the injustices of the
apartheid system include contempt, terror, brutality,
torture, fear, immorality, and massive force. When
Tekwane is arrested he is told by the detective sitting
next to him that the police will not believe any
"stories" that a "baboon" such as himself may want to
tell [p. 2]. Both arresting officers ridicule Tekwane in
anticipation of his request for a lawyer and contemptuously dismiss him as a mere "thing." They promise to make
Tekwane "shit" should he fail to provide them with sought-
after information. And true to their promise the two
officers carry out a brutal and terrifying campaign of
torture against Tekwane. After his refusal to answer the
major's question, Tekwane is hustled along a corridor to
the top of the steps leading to a basement room from
where one of the officers kicks him "so that he rolled
over and over down the stone steps, crying out, the hand-
cuffs preventing him from breaking his fall." The
officer then proceeds to "urinate off the steps into the
prisoner's face." Tekwane is then doubly handcuffed and
"thrust . . . over to a staple in the wall" where the
other end of the manacles is clicked to it. This causes
Tekwane to "choke" and "heave" as he experiences "an
awful sensation of asphyxiation and horrifying doom."
The two policemen now begin a systematic round of merci-
less beating of the hapless man [p. 7].
    The horror of Tekwane's treatment and death and the
brutal, unnecessary slaying of unarmed protesting people
at Sharpeville show that "behind the ugly mask of the
regime was an even uglier face . . ." [p. 3] of the
police who ensure the regime's survival. The "uglier
face" is very much dependent on intimidation of its victims and instilling an awesome fear that often paralyzes
the oppressed. Beukes almost runs into a "routine check"
by the police as he passes the railway station. This
near encounter with the police causes Beukes's heart to
"beat a little pronouncedly" because in South Africa
"people who were not White—even the criminally innocent
—always reacted that way." Since this is a country
where a person without knowledge could commit "a hundred
and one crimes," "palpitations of the heart had become a

national disease" [pp. 63-64]. The oppressed people who
are unnecessarily harassed by the police are treated with
provocation and utter contempt. The pass book of one of
the oppressed is demanded rudely and then the "pale white
fingers like maggots flicked over the pages, identifying
the bearer against the photograph." The policeman comments provocatively that "all you bliksems look the
blerry same. Where did your mother get you from, hey?"
Others of the oppressed are accused of carrying dagga
and generally dismissed as being "baboons" [p. 67]. This
display of contemptuous and brutal power ensures that the
oppressed do not openly challenge the unjust system of
South Africa. But it also ensures that the hatred for
the police and what they represent is complete on the
part of the oppressed.

The police as discovered in this "routine check" are
not above being immoral. One of the policemen indicates
that when he is in need of sexual satisfaction he does
not hesitate to use drunk women and "hottentots" [p. 65].
This attitude of immorality also exists in the manner in
which they intimidate some of the oppressed to act as a
"fif' column" of spies and betrayers [p. 7]. The organizers of the resistance movement are in constant fear
of the "informers" who frequent their organization. This
is how Tekwane's section is discovered and it is also the
reason why Beukes must constantly fear that a planted
link in the organization will betray his work. When Tommy returns with a "parcel" from Polsky, Beukes reveals
the suspicion and fear that he must continually experience [p. 50]. The presence of "informers" in the community stifles political dissent. Combined with a fear of
political intimidation there is an air of hopelessness
that surrounds the oppressed people. Hence, when Beukes
demonstrates to Beatie Adams that she is being exploited
by her employer, she answers as follows: "Yes, I reckon
so. But what can us people do?" Beukes's firm reply is,
"There are things people can do. . . . I'm not saying a
person can change it tomorrow or next year. But even if
you don't get what you want today, soon, it's a matter of
pride, dignity. You follow me?" [p. 11].

For many of the oppressed outrage against the
apartheid regime is expressed only when personally affected or when one of their own represents the regime.
Hence the taxi driver reacts to the Group Areas Act and
to unfair employment practices only when he is personally
affected [p. 25]. And in the bus that Beukes travels on,

anger at a system that not only decrees separate buses
for the oppressors and the oppressed but in fact provides
fewer travel facilities for a much larger public is
directed at the nonwhite conductor and not the white
owners of the bus company [pp. 68-69].

Generally, La Guma indicates, many of the oppressed
escape into their own world of cheap pleasure, fantasize
about better lives that are lived in romantic worlds, or
engage in petty class poses. For Tommy, as shown earlier, "reality, life, could be shut out by the blare of
dance-bands and the voices of crooners." When Beukes
asks Tommy whether he "bloody well sing[s] when [he is]
eating, too," he replies as follows: "Youse too serious,
ou Buke, too serious like. Me, I take things mos
easy all the time." To this reply Beukes responds, "Too
bladdy easy. . . . Too bladdy easy. There's people wor-
rying their brains out in this world and you just take it
easy." Tommy's nonchalant comment is simply, "Ah, why
worry? If you worry you die, if you don't worry you also
die" [pp. 52-53].

Like the artisans and the lower middle classes that
have succeeded in rising slightly above the living standard of the majority of their compatriots in the urban
slums and ghettoes, many of the oppressed care little
about the plight of the majority and instead wrap themselves inside a cocoon of unreality and "banality" [p.
83]. This is the sad, plastic world that Bennett's wife
has wrapped herself and Bennett in and has made him an
unreliable helper of the cause that Beukes serves. In
fear of his wife's opposition to Beukes and his meddling
in "politics," he spends his weekend on a segregated
beach and fails to keep his promise of lodging Beukes for
the weekend [p. 19].

In the face of an environment that is dominated by a
brutal police force with their cohorts of "informers" and
many members of an oppressed community who are selfish,
class-oriented, wrapped in unreality, and who turn their
frustration on each other, it seems difficult and at
times impossible to organize a resistance and liberation
movement against the racist regime. In moments of despair
and longing to be with Frances and his child, Beukes
wonders as well, "Why the hell am I doing this?" Fortunately, he abandons "the thought a little reluctantly,
discarding it like a favourite coat, and went along the
road, carrying the cheap case packed with illegal hand-
bills" [p. 71]. Beukes knows that he is a tiny but neces-

sary part of a struggle that began with the Bushmen warriors at the beginning of the Dutch invasion of South Africa in 1652. He knows that he is part of a just struggle
that has had its moments of triumph in the early wars between the blacks and whites and that must once again and
finally reach the upper hand. Hence, although the task
of defeating an "ignoble regime" is very heavy, and even
though the help needed is "as shaky as hell," it is necessary to hang on because "sometimes . . . you understand
why, often because there was nothing else to do. You
couldn't say, the hell with it, I'm going home" [p. 49].

Beukes and Tekwane's chief task is to make the oppressed aware of the reforming and revolutionary option
that is available to them. This is an option that La
Guma observes has been pursued in the past. Several
references are made to the mass political meetings and
rallies that were held before the Sharpeville uprisings.
When Isaac protests against using his lunch break to join
the other black workers in a game of cards, Sam replies,
"Ah, Ikey, <u>ou</u> pal. . . . You could <u>mos</u> take us all
down to the square in the old days to hear a meeting.
Nowadays all meetings is <u>mos</u> stopped, don't I say? All
you can hear now is them holy rollers. There's <u>mos</u>
nothing else to do" [p. 114]. Elias Tekwane remembers
his own first incursion into the resistance movement when
he joined in a mass meeting to assist the African laundry
workers who had decided to go "on strike for better
wages" [p. 133]. Beukes, Tekwane, and many others are
clandestinely preparing and delivering protest pamphlets
indicating that the security police are unable to quell
all dissent and readying the oppressed for their
inevitable struggle. After the successful mission that
is pursued with such vigor and intensity in the novel,
the newspaper headlines and stories indicate the bewilderment of the police [pp. 144-45].

The walls of the near-deserted colored suburb are
defiantly defaced with slogans such as "You Are Now
Entering The Police State," "Down With Racist Tyranny,"
and "Free Our Leaders" [pp. 24, 26]. Allusions are
repeatedly made to the military cadres "up north" [p. 22]
and at the end of the novel Isaac as "Paul" accompanied
by "Peter" and "Michael" are smuggled out of the country
by Henny April to be trained as guerrilla fighters to
come back to haunt the racist regime. The decision of
the resistance movement to meet the violence-oriented
security police on their own battle grounds is a neces-

sary and an encouraging development for Beukes: "It is a good thing that we are now working for armed struggle. It gives people confidence to think that soon they might combine mass activity with military force. One does not like facing the fascist guns like sheep." Tekwane agrees with Beukes but observes that there is still much to learn. He sees the military activity as but an extension of the nonmilitary work that has preceded it: "Step by step our people must acquire both the techniques of war and the means for fighting such a war. It is not only the advanced ones, but the entire people that must be prepared, convinced" [pp. 143-44].

The successful departure to "the north" of "Peter," "Michael," and "Paul" is a short moment of triumph for the resistance work carried out by Tekwane, Beukes, and others. But it is an essential moment that people such as Beukes, Tekwane, Flotman, and Abdullah must have to carry on their uplifting but difficult task. Hence, when one of Beukes's protégés, Isaac, turns up at Henny April's place as the guerrilla activist Paul, Beukes can hardly restrain his joy [pp. 178-79]. Isaac takes the place of Basil February, to whom the novel is dedicated, and also symbolizes to Beukes the warrior past of the oppressed, the future victory of the just struggle for liberation, and the chief reason for his task of preparing and awakening the people for the battle at hand. Hence, unlike the first three books, In the Fog of the Season's End concludes with the certain knowledge that the foggy night with its walking ghosts is about to be burned away. The final, triumphant vision of a liberated South Africa is one that Beukes can "turn back to where the children had gathered in the sunlit yard" [p. 181].

In the Fog of the Season's End is La Guma's most explicitly autobiographical work. Not only is it dedicated to one of his closest friends, but, as he says, "everyone mentioned in the novel and every incident come from my lived past" (8). In the first three books, La Guma used his work and political careers well: A Walk in the Night blends his reporter's work and his need to provide a history of the Cape colored community; in And a Threefold Cord he uses his own intimate knowledge of growing up in a ghetto; and The Stone Country covers inevitably some of the considerable time he has spent in prison for opposing the racist regime. In this last novel, as indicated earlier, he sees himself as George Adams

providing a telescopic view of the events. In the Fog
of the Season's End is a very intimate and detailed portrait of resistance work, one that is spiritually and physically embedded in La Guma's psyche and bodily person.

The depiction of Beukes and his arduous work is large-
ly a portrait of Alex La Guma and his work. By looking
closely at how Beukes operates, the reader obtains not
only a good insight into resistance work but, especially,
into how La Guma functioned in his political work in
South Africa. The places that appear in the novel are
colored suburbs of Cape Town with the exception of the
black township Langa, where Tekwane is arrested and
Beukes wounded and the "expensive" white Cape Town suburb
where Beukes wanders around and witnesses a carefree
social gathering. Again there is the slow but restless
movement through the ghostly night; but unlike Adonis,
who chooses not to struggle against injustice, Beukes is
bent on destroying the fog of cruelty and oppression.
His wanderings give the reader an excellent panoramic
view of the colored suburbs and community, and magnificent recordings of dialogue.

The characters are real figures who worked with the
writer in the resistance struggle. Elias Tekwane's name
is fictitious, and so are the names of Flotman, Polsky,
Abdullah, Isaac, Tommy, Henny April, Halima, and Beatie
Adams. But the roles they play in the novel are the
actual ones they performed and are still performing. La
Guma says the following about this aspect:

> I knew these people. They were my friends. They
> came from all walks of life. Every race. Every
> religion. We worked together. And when one of us was
> arrested, we were all worried. But we knew we had to
> carry on, come what may. I am proud to have been
> associated with them. And I think one can say that
> this story is my way of remembering them. Thanking
> them. (9)

But La Guma refuses to reveal their names because of
security reasons, since many are still living and carrying on the struggle in South Africa (10).

La Guma refers to several incidents that occurred in
his own life: his first, personal experience with race
discrimination at the circus; the school concert where
they prepare themselves to sing at a white school; his
experience as a factory worker; his stint at the American

oil company where Isaac works; and the meeting and courting of Frances, although he did not marry this girl in his own life [pp. 40, 83-84, 41, 110, 34]. But the father of Frances in the novel and his interest in rugby are part of his history with Blanche Hermans, the woman whom La Guma married in 1954 [p. 93]. Beukes's frequent absences from his home to carry on his political work and to escape the dragnet of the security police are directly from La Guma's life experience. Although La Guma was never wounded, the doctor who treats Beukes "is still very much alive in Cape Town" (12). And as La Guma indicates, the despair and joy and the fear and hope that Beukes expresses "are straight out of my own life history" (13).

The autobiographical nature of In the Fog of the Season's End makes this book La Guma's most explicit statement on the sociopolitical situation as it exists in South Africa. There is less of the slight, ironic allusion here. It is more direct and powerful. The sides in the battle are drawn clearly and the result is more certain. This stance does not weaken the book, as David Rabkin suggests (14). In fact, La Guma shows a natural progression, and it blends art and his committed beliefs extremely well. Altogether, as Gerald Moore notes, this is his most "mature" novel to date, and as Leonard Kibera argues, it is "a major achievement in African literature" (15).

Chapter Seven
A Time for Cleansing:
Time of the Butcherbird

Time of the Butcherbird was published in 1979 in London
by Heinemann. It is the first of La Guma's five long
books that was conceived and written in its entirety
outside South Africa. Free of constant harassment and
surveillance by the South African security police and now
able to place all of his energies behind the struggle of
the Liberation Movement in exile, La Guma is able in this
novel to address a central question of South African
society in a more defiant way. He explains his objective
in the following statement:

> In the other novels I have shown that there are so
> many aspects to South African life. If one is to give
> a good picture of South Africa one must deal with some
> of these aspects. I believe that one of the most
> serious social problems of South Africa is that of
> mass removal of millions of African people from their
> well-established homes and the government program to
> establish or reinforce "Bantustans." In addition, of
> course, it is not only the fact of the "Bantustans"
> but also the attitude of the people and the resistance
> that's been put up on various levels in the rural
> areas to this policy. When the idea of writing a
> novel on this came to me, I thought it was necessary
> to combine the effect of the "Bantustans" and the
> resistance of the people. (1)

The novel is dedicated "To The Dispossessed" (2). The
question of being dispossessed of ancestral lands goes
back to the very beginning of the European invasion of
South Africa in 1652. What started off as an experiment
by the Dutch East Indies Company to use the Cape of Good
Hope as a halfway-house, a refreshment station for their
sailors and traders on their lucrative trade journeys to
the East, soon turned into the establishment of a coloni-
alist settlement that brutally and forcibly dispossessed

the indigenous population of their ancestral land. By
the early 1930s the minority population laid claim to 87
percent of the land and its resources. In the face of
militant cries from the dispossessed black population and
urgent entreaties from the minority regime's overseas
friends, the South African government enacted in 1959 the
National Homelands Policy, which has since been referred
to in a derogatory manner as the "Bantustans" policy.
This act of Parliament reiterated the claim of the white
population and set aside the remaining 13 percent of the
land for the majority black population. Furthermore,
this portion of South Africa was divided into thirteen
pieces of land and was to be occupied along tribal lines.
Hence, whether a black person was born in this designated territory or not, the government could at the
stroke of a pen or with the help of bulldozers and police
vans remove thousands of black people to corroded,
deserted areas of South Africa. Since the passage of the
act, millions of blacks have been cruelly affected and
towns such as Limehill, Dimbaza, and Stinkgat have become
the homes of malnourished, unemployed, diseased, and brow-
beaten people. Time of the Butcherbird deals in the
first place with this tragic question.

    A second objective that La Guma has in mind is to
"deal with the attitudes of the white community to this
issue of mass removals and to study their attitude to
blacks as a whole" (3). In A Walk in the Night and
And a Threefold Cord, La Guma had set out consciously
to write about his own colored community with the understanding that this community's trials, tribulations, and
triumphs had been ignored in the larger portrait of South
Africa. In In the Fog of the Season's End, the reader
is introduced to the black community, but most of the
characters are colored and most of the places where the
action occurs are in colored sections of Cape Town. In
Time of the Butcherbird, the colored community has disappeared and the two chief contending groups with their
specific characters are black and white. La Guma describes this occurrence as follows:

> As I informed you before, I tried to draw pictures of
> the coloured people in my earlier books. Having dealt
> with them to a certain extent, I then turned to other
> scenes in our society. I started in In the Fog of
> the Season's End where we not only have coloured
> people but the rest of the society comes into the

picture.   In Time of the Butcherbird I discuss the
various communities in the country and their relationship. (4)

As indicated earlier, Time of the Butcherbird is the
only book to date that La Guma conceived and wrote entirely outside South Africa.   Here as in all the previous
novels the writer's characteristic technique of portraying character against a social background is noticeable.
But what is missing in this book is the character or two
who come directly from the writer's own life experiences.
In this sense, then, this novel is the least autobiographical and it gives rise to the treatment of character
and story in a more symbolic way.   This is how La Guma
sees this new development:

> The characters in the novel are more symbolic than the
> characters in the other novels, I suppose because the
> characters in the previous novels are people whom I
> knew directly.   Here I portrayed people whom I hoped
> were representative of the South African scene.   I
> collected enough scenes of South Africa—"Bantustans,"
> praying for rain, people in the desert, and then I
> wrote.   I tried to combine symbolism, character and
> action.   (5)

In his characteristic manner, La Guma has in an
economical and succinct manner succeeded to pack together
in Time of the Butcherbird two major stories and a
number of shorter ones.   The major stories are tied
integrally to the theme of the time of the butcherbird
and deal with the personal revenge of Shilling Murile and
the forced mass removal of the blacks and their resistance to this occurrence.   The minor stories, and in some
cases more personal portraits than stories, deal with the
failed marriage of Edgar Stopes and Maisie Barends, the
history of Oupa Meulen, the struggle between Hlangeni and
Mma-Tau, and the dismal failure to establish harmonious
and just relationships between blacks and whites on both
the personal and collective levels.   All of these
stories, major and minor, are held together by the
metaphor of the butcherbird.   The butcherbird is common
in South Africa and is found especially in areas where
there are cattle, sheep, and pigs.   These livestock are
generally molested by bloodsucking insects known as
"ticks" in South Africa.   The butcherbird preys on these

parisites, and in performing this noble task it is considered by rural dwellers as a bird of good omen that
cleanses nature of negative influences. The book, as La
Guma indicates, is, therefore, a testimony to his belief
that the time of cleansing South Africa's negative ways
has come:

> The title of the novel comes from African folklore.
> One of the riddles from the oral tradition indicates
> that the butcherbird represents something which not
> only cleanses the cattle but also cleanses the socie-
> ty. It does away with the wizards, the sorcerers, and
> those people who have a negative effect on the socie-
> ty. What I'm trying to say is that conscious resis-
> tance of the people heralds the time when the
> butcherbird will cleanse South Africa of racism,
> oppression, and so on. (6)

Shilling Murile's revenge of his brother's death
occupies a large part of the story. The stalking and
killing of Hannes Meulen satisfy a part of the role of
the butcherbird. But the butcherbird's destruction of
parasites satisfies the entire population that live off
the livestock. Murile, on the other hand, seeks at first
personal revenge, and even though his action brings to an
end the cruel and ignoble life of Meulen, he does not see
his task as benefiting all those who have suffered at the
hands of Meulen. When he finally joins forces with the
collective struggle he becomes an integral part of the
butcherbird's essential work of cleansing the society of
parasites. Murile hails from a family that has lived in
the Karoo since before the invasion of the Europeans. As
a grown-up, Murile is employed by Hannes Meulen, who is
an Afrikaner and a big sheep farmer of the area. On the
occasion of Meulen's sister Berta's wedding, "extra
kaffirs were needed to help with the menial chores of the
celebration" [p. 67]. One of the "extra" blacks (the
term kaffir is used by the whites in a derogatory
manner against blacks; although it can have several meanings, its chief denotation is that of subhuman) is
Murile's younger brother, Timi. During the course of the
wedding celebration the black servants help themselves to
large doses of wine and by early evening both Murile and
Timi are intoxicated. In their intoxicated state they
decide that the sheep should also participate in the celebration by dancing [p. 72]. The result of this drunken

action is the panic escape of the sheep from the kraal.

Shilling and Timi's playful but irresponsible action leads to a tragic end. Hannes Meulen and his farm fore-man, Dawie Opperman, discover the deed and track the brothers down. Opperman observes the drunken state of the men and suggests to Meulen that the men be taken "to the police-station" and be charged [p. 73]. Meulen insists instead that they be tied to the fence post and be left there overnight. Since it is in the middle of the cold winter, the prospect of tying up and leaving the two brothers creates dismay in Opperman. But Meulen, in his contempt for the blacks, ignores Opperman's concern. The impaling of the men by Meulen imitates the action of the butcherbird and is even seen by him as an act of cleansing his community from "baboons." But since it is Meulen and his Afrikaner community who have lived cruelly off the backs of blacks, La Guma indicates to the reader to be careful of assigning loose meanings to the butcher-bird.

During the cold night Timi dies of exposure. His death is not discovered by Murile until the next morning when Opperman and Meulen reappear to "untie these two baboons." Meulen's heartless reaction to Opperman's discovery of Timi's death is "Dammit. . . . These kaffirs are always causing trouble" [p. 76]. When Opperman's words finally register with Murile, he stag-gers to his feet and with "the neck of the broken wine bottle" he slashes Opperman's left forearm, "opening it to the bone so that he screamed with pain, staring at the belching blood." Murile is then clubbed on his skull by the butt of Meulen's shotgun. In the white district court Murile has the charge of "sheep-stealing" dropped against him but he is "sentenced to ten years of hard labour" for "attempted murder of Opperman." Hannes Meulen is given "a severe reprimand and a stiff fine" for causing Timi's death [p. 77].

The revenge story of Shilling Murile begins after he has served eight years in prison. His mission is to kill Hannes Meulen and, consequently, he is unimpressed by his ancestral landscape. His only conscious thought is that "I am not long for this place" [p. 14]. He shares in the singleminded purpose of an ant he observes, and this rein-forces his resolve. The comparison of human action to the action of the insect is characteristic of La Guma's use of metaphor. Often he looks to the animal kingdom. This can be found in the incident of the drowning fly in

And a Threefold Cord, the valiant mouse in The Stone
Country, and, of course, the butcherbird in this novel.
La Guma admires Murile's singlemindedness; but, since he
is cast in the role of the butcherbird, Murile must not
only be singleminded in purpose but must also expand
beyond the ant and become the utilitarian bird of
cleansing.

In his brooding, seemingly self-sufficient world of
revenge, Murile refuses kind offers of friendship as in
the case of the old shepherd, Madonele, and Mma-Tau, the
militant sister of the headman, Hlangeni. Even though
Madonele recognizes Murile for the boy "who had zest"
when he was growing up, Murile is taciturn and keeps his
own counsel. His only response is, "It is better to
remember and to wait, rather than to talk." But Murile
admits to himself that one cannot escape the history of
one's ancestral home; after all, he asks rhetorically,
"Is not my brother buried here?" In this query and his
statement that "the people have lived here since the time
of our grandfathers" [pp. 19-21], it is noticeable that
Murile is not as singleminded as he appears. The soften-
ing process continues when Murile meets Mma-Tau, who
lectures him on the subject of personal revenge and collective struggle [p. 80]. Mma-Tau ends her conversation
by urging Murile to use his "strong" personal "hatred" on
behalf of the collectivity:

You can be of use to us. You have hatred, strong
hatred, the desire to find justice. But do not be
satisfied with your personal achievement of justice,
if you find it. It is a small thing when compared
with the people's need for justice. As I have said, a
man with your desire for vengeance belongs with the
people. [p. 80]

The strong words from Mma-Tau have an impact on
Murile, because after he kills Meulen and Stopes he
returns to join the collective struggle against the
unjust Afrikaner forces. But for the moment he dismisses
Mma-Tau's counsel as the "trumpets . . . of a she-
elephant" and insists once more that "I have matters of
my own to attend to" [p. 84].

The theme of Murile as part butcherbird of the first
story unfolds now in a purposeful manner. Hannes Meulen
and what he represents can be considered to be the bloodsucking "ticks" or insects that molest Murile and the

black population. It is Meulen through his abusive treatment of the blacks who prevents any possibility of establishment of a society that respects all its people. In
the second main story dealing with the mass removal of
blacks it is Meulen, representing the interests of
Afrikaner businessmen, who negotiates with mining
investors and government authorities the forcible dispossession of black ancestral land. Meulen, in the oral
tradition of the butcherbird, is, therefore, the negative
force that survives parasitically on the backs of blacks.
Until now he has been able to succeed in his actions;
but with the conscious return of Murile, the avenging
butcherbird, and the awareness of Mma-Tau's supporters
that they and those before them have been duped for
centuries, the parasitic actions of Meulen and his followers are about to face the cleansing time of the butcherbird.

The butcherbird is not a noisy bird, and it goes about
its task determinedly and singlemindedly. This is the
reason why Murile's intentions are not revealed openly
and boastfully to Madonele or Mma-Tau. In the same way
as the butcherbird is watchful of the guile of its prey,
so, too, does Murile pay attention to all the events that
surround Meulen. La Guma's magnificent power to draw
detailed, alive characters comes to the fore well in his
description of Murile. The reader first observes the
protagonist while he is "sitting with his feet in the
ditch at the side of the road." He wears "a khaki army
shirt, washed many times and worn out at the collar, and
almost colourless denim trousers, badly frayed at the
cuffs and spotted with old stains." In a nonchalant but
purposeful manner he slings "his jacket over a shoulder"
and plods off, "trailing the cloud of dust, apparently
oblivious of the sun overhead that turned the light of
the world about him a cruel brass-yellow." To show his
militant intentions, La Guma tells us that "the jacket
was a cast-off top of khaki serge battledress, one of its
epaulettes dangled free and an elbow had been torn" [pp.
13-14]. Then the writer proceeds to give a detailed
portrait of the restless, singleminded character [p. 16].

The parasite "tick" or insect Meulen is described
equally well by the writer. As indicated earlier, in
this novel La Guma for the first time makes a conscious
effort to draw characters from outside the colored community, and hence it is worth watching whether he is able
to bring the same authenticity to bear as he did earlier.

In discussing this issue with La Guma, he observes that
in South Africa one has several ways of obtaining information about how whites and blacks live and react to situations. There is the general view that comes to one
through the news media. Since the races cannot be kept
entirely away from each other, there is an opportunity to
observe people on the street, in stores, on sports
fields, and so on. For the politically active such as La
Guma, there are those white and black South Africans who
are linked with coloreds and Indians in the same antiracist struggle. Further opportunities for La Guma to
observe and assess the behavior of whites and blacks came
through visits to the rural areas and through the South
African education system. Finally, says La Guma, in 1955
he was detained by the police in the Karoo as he was on
his way to the Congress of the People in Johannesburg and
he had a good opportunity to observe the Afrikaners in
this area (7). In developing the story of Hannes Meulen
as the bloodsucking "tick," La Guma provides the reader
with a masterful account of Afrikaner history as seen
through three generations of one family. In an intimate,
detailed, and believable manner the writer traces Afrikaner history from the nineteenth century with Oupa
Meulen and brings us to the present day with his grandson
Hannes Meulen. As an outsider to the Afrikaner tradition, La Guma is probably the most successful South
African writer to penetrate the laager, and this
ensures for him a reputation of being an extremely perceptive and imaginative observer of the psyche of the
Afrikaner community.

The history of the Meulens in the Karoo begins with
Oupa Johannes Meulen, who after the Boer War decided to
settle there and establish his ancestral roots. Oupa
Meulen is very old when the reader meets him and he is
disinterested in the present, remembering only the old
days of glory, so that "gradually he had withdrawn into a
sort of private world of his own, a world which existed
only in his disintegrating mind, a perpetual dream" [p.
58]. La Guma captures in a brilliant and authentic
manner the old man when he sums him up as follows:
"Dried out and stringy, Oupa Meulen was as bloodless and
tough as biltong, the jerked meat he had lived on for
most of his early years, and seemed almost stubbornly to
refuse to leave this earth." Oupa Meulen does not recognize his grandchildren as descendants of his because
their ways are so different from his own. While the

wedding feast of his granddaughter is being celebrated,
the old man's mind wanders off to earlier days when Afrikaners assembled for feasts with their "ox-wagons and
Cape-carts." In this exercise of memory La Guma intro-
duces us cleverly to the peculiar clothing, mannerisms,
and sounds and smells of the Afrikaners of earlier times.
Rejecting the new ways of his granddaughter's wedding,
Oupa Meulen remembers his own wedding day, when he and
his wife stepped "solemnly up onto the stoep, into the
house and the marriage chamber with the decked-out bed
and the chairs where they sit while each guest, clad in
old-fashioned Sunday clothes preserved in wooden kists
[chests] for such occasions, is individually introduced
to them, to wish them happiness, to kiss the bride and
groom." He remembers the dishes of "lamb, pumpkin,
string-beans," the drinking of "brandy," the "fiddle and
concertina," and "the young couples whirling and skipping
while bearded old men and bonneted women look on from the
sidelines, feet tapping" [pp. 67-68, 69, 70].

Oupa Meulen does not accept the presence of the blacks
in South Africa, nor does it disturb him that the land
that the Afrikaners possess has been forcibly stolen from
the blacks. His only contact with a black person is the
loyal master-slave relationship with Koos, who is as old
as Oupa Meulen and lives in the back of the crumbling
farmhouse. Faithful to the end, Koos is prepared to
forget all the cruelty and insults that whites such as
Oupa Meulen have unleashed against blacks, and thus he
pleads with Murile to spare the old man because he has
been "kind" to him [p. 94].

Christofel Meulen, the son of Oupa Meulen, remembers
the history of his people but is less inclined to live in
the past. He is adept at sheep farming but he "also had
other interests in life." Christofel Meulen loves the
land and to him country is "not only a geographical
entity, an anthem, celebrations of Dingane's Day, the day
of Blood River." For him country is "a matter of who
owns the flat, dreary red and yellow plains and the low,
undulating hills, the grass and the water" [p. 57].
Convinced by his conception of his and the Afrikaners'
place in life, Christofel ensures the upbringing of his
children in a Calvinistic, Afrikaner manner. Church
every Sunday, being dressed up in black kisklere
("funeral") clothes; the meetings of men on Saturdays in
the schoolhouse with their riding-breeches and gray
shirts; the support of Germany in the Second World War;

the belief that Germans stood against miscegenation
and bastardization, ideas that the British and Jews
support; and, finally, the raising of right arms and
hands by the men at the meeting as they proclaim that
"the Afrikan- der volk is not the work of man, but the
work of God" [p. 58].

Christofel Meulen dies when Hannes Meulen is fifteen
years old and the responsibility of the farm and the
children is passed on to Johannes Meulen. But Oupa
Meulen is disinterested in both farm and children and
this provides Hannes Meulen with the opportunity to carve
out his own destiny. Like his father before him, Meulen
is interested in more than the managing of the farm. But
not only does he become successful as a public man—being
elected to represent the Karoo constituency in the white
national Parliament—but he is now cast in the role of
being the representative of the Afrikaner capitalists'
interests. When the reader first meets the "handsome,"
affable Meulen, he has just returned from a meeting with
government authorities to ensure the mass removal of the
blacks so that the local Afrikaner businessmen, including
his future father-in-law, Kasper Steen, and the mining
investors can possess and exploit the resources of the
land. He is now "near forty" and a graduate of an Afrikaner university, a modern Afrikaner who is ready to
continue to dispossess the blacks of their heritage. He
looks upon blacks as "baboons" and "kaffirs" and is contemptuous of any "stirring" by blacks for better wages
and rights. He sees these demands as a threat to Afrikaner Kultuur ("culture") and honor, and parroting his
father he argues as well that "the Afrikaner people is
not the work of man, it is the work of God." He takes
exception to the Afrikaners' "overseas friends" for sug-
gesting change—"Can we believe in ourselves if we also
allow ourselves to be influenced by the changing way of
life in their countries?"--and argues that the Afrikaners' strength and purity are dependent on their un-
flinching stand against "liberalism" and change [p. 64].

The three generations of Meulens parallel the development of the Afrikaner community. Until 1833, when the
Great Trek of Dutch settlers from the Cape of Good Hope
to the inland areas of South Africa occurred, the settler
community considered itself but an extension of the Dutch
ancestors from which it derived. But the many wars the
settlers engaged in with the blacks and the English led
them to a belief in a God-given destiny. They now began

to see themselves as Afrikaners, children of Africa and
not Europe, and took pride in the language of Afrikaans,
which they had originally discarded as the language of
their colored servants or kombuis taal ("kitchen
language"). The Afrikaner generation of Johannes Meulen
forcibly robbed the blacks of their ancestral land and
stole their sheep and cattle and later defended their
stolen wealth against the English in the Boer War.
Although defeated, the English did not ask the Afrikaners
to return the stolen land to the blacks and, hence, they
built their society on ill-gotten gains. The generation
of Christofel Meulen, freed of further wars against the
English and the blacks, consolidated their gains and
believed even more firmly in the destiny of the Afrikaner
nation. All of these aspects are inherited by Hannes
Meulen's generation: a more modern, better educated
group who still have contempt for the blacks but who
desire now to strip the blacks of more ancestral land so
as to develop their new, capitalistic interests. In this
regard, then, Hannes Meulen is the composite representative of the Afrikaner "ticks" that have preyed on the
backs of the blacks for a very long time.

The time of the butcherbird finally comes when Murile
visits the Meulen farm looking for both Hannes Meulen and
Jaap Opperman. He discovers that Opperman has died and
that Meulen is in town. Murile takes one of Meulen's
automatic shotguns and proceeds to the hotel in town. He
arrives soon after the Afrikaner prayer service for rain
and kills the "tick" who has plagued him and his people
in the past [p. 110]. He also kills Edgar Stopes by
accident, but this death is an indication by La Guma that
he considers the English-speaking, white South African
not less blameworthy of sucking the blood of blacks: the
time of the butcherbird has come for this part of the
white population as well.

Murile, having completed his personal mission, now
joins Mma-Tau in the collective black struggle of
cleansing South Africa of racism, injustice, and oppression. Murile is the type of character La Guma has been
moving toward since the portrayal of Michael Adonis in A
Walk in the Night. Adonis recognizes the "tick" but
chooses not to challenge it and instead joins another
negative group of society. Charlie Pauls in And a Threefold Cord is aware that it is because of the white,
racist, class structure that he and his people are
oppressed, but, apart from the personal satisfaction of

hitting a policeman, he is unable to do anything about the situation. George Adams in The Stone Country is defiant and he organizes the community in political protest action, but this is not enough because the "tick" society arrests those who challenge their hegemony. In In the Fog of the Season's End La Guma peoples the book with types such as Tekwane, Beukes, Flotman, and Isaac, who organize political action against the regime—defiant people but not yet ready to carry out the mission of the butcherbird. Murile becomes that character and he completes his mission very well.

The second major narrative deals with the forced removal of blacks. The novel opens with a depressing but beautifully described passage of what happens when blacks are evicted from their ancestral land:

> The dust settled slowly on the metal of the tank and on the surface of the brackish water it contained, laboriously pumped from below the sand; on the rough cubist mounds of folded and piled tents dumped there by officialdom; on the sullen faces of the people who had been unloaded like the odds and ends of furniture they had been allowed to bring with them, powdering them grey and settling in the perspiring lines around mouths and in the eye sockets, settling on the unkempt and travel-creased clothes, so that they had the look of scarecrows left behind, abandoned in this place. [p. 1]

These are the remnants of once proud people who have now lost their ancestral land to satisfy the racist and capitalist longings of the ruling white minority of South Africa. These followers of Hlangeni, the headman, have been brow-beaten so as to accept the usual whiteman's solution to the robbery of their land. And, as La Guma indicates, the pattern of dispossession is as familiar as when it first happened. There is first of all the decision by the local Afrikaner businessmen, in this case working in harmony with the mining investors, that they need the land. The business arrangement is explained by Hannes Meulen to Kasper Steen: "They [the mining corporation] will set up the company, fifty-two percent held by the government through them and the other forty-eight will be offered to the public. I, of course, pointed out that you and I are interested in buying a substantial amount of those shares." To secure the land

Meulen acts on the "request of the [Afrikaner] people" to move the "kaffirs." This request is filtered through the local Afrikaner magistrate and chief commissioner and a favorable decision is made by the Department of Community Affairs. The point of this official exercise is to convince an immoral people that they have acted in a just and "moral" way. The Department of Community Affairs then arranges "with the railways for a train to take them [the blacks] from here" and "the local farmers" are asked to "supply lorries to bring them [the blacks] to the station . . ." [p. 61].

As so often in the past, many blacks are still not fully convinced that the whites are "ticks" who will only listen once the blacks remove them forcibly from their backs. Since they believe in reason and justice, a delegation of two, led by Kobe, is despatched to speak to the chief commissioner. Before the two men enter the commissioner's office, the reader is given a good, general insight into the treatment of blacks by white officialdom. The commissioner's clerk "scowls" at them because they are black and refers to their "usual kaffir smell." The commissioner as well "did not go near because fastidiously he too wished to avoid the odour of travel that clung to them." When told of their mission, the commissioner at first refuses to speak to them because they are not the "headman" Hlangeni, but then in a sharp, magisterial tone he berates them as children for assuming that the white authority would change its decision. Kobe informs the commissioner that this will not be the last time he will hear from them on this issue. But the commissioner dismisses this ominous warning as "a lot of nonsense" [pp. 10-11, 12, 13].

The discussion between the commissioner and the black delegation is merely a repetition of what has also transpired between the parties since the Afrikaners robbed the blacks of their land. In earlier times the conquest simply occurred through the Afrikaners' belief in the Bible and the musket. In a more modern age, where such action could be frowned upon by the Afrikaners' overseas friends, there is a need to devise sham outlets of communication between the groups. In earlier times the blacks defended their ancestral lands in fierce battles and were defeated only when superior armed power was employed. But a period ensued when the chiefs and elders of the black community permitted through offers of personal privilege the giving up of rights of their people

without opposition. Hlangeni, who was a chief but had
been demoted by the whites to the inferior position of
headman, is now ready once again quietly to forfeit the
ancestral land of his people. But many of his followers
disagree with this view and, as in former times, they
insist on opposing the decision of the whites. This is
why it is not Hlangeni who represents their position
before the commissioner, and, furthermore, even though
Kobe expects the answer he receives from the commissioner, he has the satisfaction of having delivered the forth-
right message of the people in a firm manner.

The black people of the Karoo are now at a crossroad;
they must either be prepared to become butcherbirds and
remove the Afrikaner bloodsuckers from their backs or,
once more, permit the centuries-old injustice to continue. The first full mention and explanation of the
meaning of the butcherbird comes at this crucial time.
In some ways Shilling Murile is foreshadowing the discussion and result of the meeting of the black people when
he asks Madonele if he "knows the butcherbird." Madonele
then informs us that the butcherbird "is a hunter and
smeller-out of sorcerers, because he impales insects." A
meeting is called by Hlangeni at sunset—he is not the
proud descendant of a great people any longer, but "a
dwindling old man in a dusty black suit in spite of the
heat." Since the white authority arbitrarily demoted him
to headman, he has become "unsure," "surrounded by doubt,
trying to clasp at the cloak of old dignity that was
wearing thin." But in his speech to his assembled people
Hlangeni remembers earlier times when his people were
proud warriors and when they not only owned their land
but could roam freely about. Hlangeni goes on to argue
that "the evil that comes from his [the whiteman's] laws
and guns and money is not ours" and describes their laws
as the cause of hatred among the groups. Because
Hlangeni fears the weapons of the Afrikaners, he urges
ignoble surrender [pp. 42-45].

Hlangeni's call for surrender is accepted by some of
his followers and they emphasize this position by breaking out in "funeral" songs. But there are many others in
the community who find the stirring words of resistance
from Mma-Tau, Hlangeni's sister, easier to support. Mma-
Tau contends that while it is true that the white man has
closed his heart to brotherhood with the blacks, the
heart of the black man, however, has not been closed.
She argues further that not only does South Africa suffer

from lack of brotherhood but there is also a class struggle that divides people between rich and poor. Insisting
that "I shall not go from this land," Mma-Tau informs her
brother that the time of the butcherbird has arrived and
the onslaught must be carried out [pp. 45-48].

The small number of followers of Hlangeni obey the
instructions of the white authority and arrive in the
"wretched and deserted land" described earlier [p. 1].
The rest, under the leadership of Mma-Tau, barricade themselves and await the sergeant and his convoy of farm
lorries. Being used to meek and resigned blacks, the
sergeant refuses at first to accept Mma-Tau's authority
or the decision to disobey "the orders from the government." Annoyed at the songs of resistance, the sergeant
"unbuttons his pistol holster" and this causes a black
youth to "hurl a stone at" him. The stone misses the
sergeant, but his clerk panics and begins to flee. This
action creates fear and confusion among the drivers in
the convoy and they decide to drive away from the scene.
Red-faced and embarrassed, the sergeant wonders "who
would have thought that these bloody kaffirs would start
something like this?" And yet, not convinced as yet by
the militant action of the blacks, he views the resistance as a defeat "by a lot of baboons in jumble-sale
clothing" [p. 112]. And to confirm their determination
not to permit the "ticks" to continue to suck their blood
without resistance, stones are thrown at the sergeant and
his convoy.

The sergeant returns to the town to seek reinforce-
ments, while the black people, led by Mma-Tau, move into
the hills to continue their resistance to enslavement, as
Madonele indicates. At this point, Murile, who had
completed his personal mission earlier, joins the resistance movement and smiles because now his gun will be
used as part of the collective struggle to cleanse the
society of negative "ticks" and sorcerers. He recognizes
that the time for the butcherbird has truly arrived. The
final three paragraphs contrast sharply with the opening
of the book: gone is the hopelessness of the opening
scene where Hlangeni and the remnant of his followers
await their ultimate and despairing death as they succumb
to the cruel laws of the white society. As the "yellow-
ing afternoon light puts a golden colour on the land," a
"flight of birds swoop overhead towards a water-hole" [p.
119]. The symbolism is clear: the drought of human
destruction and unjust dispossession of land has ended,

and now the butcherbird will smell out the sorcerer, hunt
him down, and cleanse the society of his bloodsucking,
negative nature.

As indicated earlier, the three generations of Meulens
parallel in a representative manner the development of
Afrikaner history in South Africa, But since one of La
Guma's stated purposes in this novel is to present deep
and authentic insight into the Afrikaner population, he
makes mention of several more fundamental character
traits of this segment of the South African white community. From the beginning of their invasion of South
Africa, the Afrikaners have been rural, farming people;
and even today, when there is a stong element of moderni-
zation, the Afrikaners remain basically a farming community that is attached to family and church. For the men in
the rural areas the day is given over to farming activities and the weekday evenings to pleasurable gatherings
at the "taproom" of the local hotel. So as not to forget
their past the hotel lobby carries portraits of their
state president and Boer commandos who fought against the
English in the Boer War. The chief amusements for these
Afrikaner men are beer-drinking and the game of "finger-
pulling."

The Afrikaner women are excluded from the evening
rituals at the hotel; in fact they participate only in
public events that relate strictly to family matters.
Women are responsible for the moral standards of the
family and especially for the upbringing of the children.
And they are seen as the faithful, obedient helpmates of
their husbands. The role of woman as mother of the
Afrikaner male's children, the belief in a predetermined,
God-given destiny, and the insistence on the purity of
the race and the nonmingling of the Afrikaners with other
groups in South Africa are fundamental tenets of the
Afrikaners' Dutch Reformed Church. From the beginning of
the invasion and settlement of South Africa, this church
has kept a tight rein over its members' thought and
behavior. The head of the church is the dominee, or
minister, who is regarded as the wise spiritual, and
often political, leader. It is to the dominee that the
Afrikaner takes his joys, despairs, hopes, and failures.

It is the dominee's and the Afrikaner's belief that
they are the chosen people of God and that South Africa
is the Jerusalem that has been promised to them. This
Jerusalem, they contend, is now drought-stricken because
"the inhabitants" have sinned against God. The dominee

enumerates the "sins" to be the "corruption in our
cities," "lewd and lustful so-called art pictures,"
nudity in public places, suicide among teenagers, and the
use of "hallucinatory drugs." Dominee Visser is especially against "blood pollution and the lowering of the
racial level which goes with it." He urges his followers
to withstand the "Philistines" and to protect the land
against the "heathen" [pp. 106-7]. And in the square the
farm-trucks with their church-going men are prepared to
remove the blacks forcibly and unjustly from their ancestral land. In a spirit of unconcern for the rights of
others the Afrikaner community plunges headlong into
deceit and hypocrisy, believing blindly but wrongly in a
destiny designed by a merciful and forgiving God. As a
community, then, the Afrikaners are "ticks" that feed
unfairly off the blacks and can only be cleansed by the
positive action of the butcherbird.

The Afrikaner community receives most of La Guma's
attention because it dominates most aspects of South
Africa's political and social existence. Since the
writer, however, is attempting an evaluation of the attitude of the entire white community toward the blacks, the
English-speaking whites must be considered as well. The
story of Edgar Stopes and Maisie Barends is therefore
more than that of a marriage that has failed or simply a
dramatic device to link Stopes's accidental death at the
hands of Shilling Murile with the deliberate death of
Hannes Meulen. In all of La Guma's books he has
attempted to give the reader a commentary on South
Africa's history as seen from his oppressed vantage
point. Throughout Time of the Butcherbird he examines
various realities and myths of the groups that populate
South Africa. One of the myths is the belief that the
so-called liberal, English-speaking white South African
has a "better," more "meaningful" attitude to blacks.
According to this belief the settlement of South Africa
by people from the United Kingdom since 1820 brought a
more enlightened and liberal approach to the racial battle between blacks and whites. Furthermore, the view is
that racial animosities heightened after the election of
the Afrikaner Nasionale party in 1948. South African
history, however, will indicate that draconian laws such
as residential and group areas divisions, the hated pass
book laws, job discrimination, educational inequalities,
and many more unjust practices were introduced in the
days when the settlers of the United Kingdom dominated

the legislative and executive structures of South Africa.
The Nasionale party decided in 1948 and onward to
tighten the restrictions of these laws, and with the help
of many new ones the Afrikaners built up their much-
maligned apartheid system. The English settler has since
taken a disinterested back seat in solving the racial
problems of South Africa, preferring instead to mock the
Afrikaners' approach and to blame all disharmony on the
government. Meanwhile, English settler businessmen have
played and continue to play a major role in the economic
success that South Africa enjoys. In this regard they
make full use of the cheap and docile black labor gained
through the laws of apartheid, and in Time of the
Butcherbird, as part of their search for new wealth,
they continue with local Afrikaner businessmen to dispossess the blacks of their ancestral land.

The reader observes in the novel that the English-
speaking whites do not differ much in their contempt for
blacks. Not only does Edgar Stopes dislike the Afrikaners, but at the Karoo hotel where he stays he considers Fanie, the black houseboy, to be less than human
[p. 22]. Stopes's wife, Maisie, is the daughter of a
shopkeeper in an inner-city suburb chiefly inhabited by
blacks. Although he lives off the backs of these inhabitants, Barends describes them in derogatory language as
"coolies [Indians] and coloureds and the bloody China-
men." And his brother castigates him for "wasting" his
life among "bloody coolies and coons." Mrs. Barends
keeps Maisie indoors all day "because all the children in
the neighbourhood were a lot of coons." This type of
upbringing results in Maisie's describing blacks as "a
lot of niggers" and refusing to admit to her friends
where she lives because it is "right on the edge of
coolieland." And Stopes blames the poverty-stricken condition of the blacks on their "stupidity" [pp. 30-36].

Through the story of the failed marriage of Edgar and
Maisie Stopes the writer provides a good portrait of the
shabby, boring, aimless life-style of the urban, middle-
class English settlers. La Guma indicates that it is
only because of their skin color that these settlers
enjoy rights and privileges that are superior to those of
the blacks. Like the "poor-white" Mostert in And a
Threefold Cord, they have been deceived by their leaders
to believe that they are superior to the blacks. Hence,
to keep this illusion they tend to be openly racist
toward the blacks. Although privileged, this class of

people fails to benefit from the many opportunities
offered. The children, as noted in the case of Maisie,
are bored by school and tend to drop out early. With
little interest in occupying meaningful working positions, many of them live in the fantasy world of Holly-
wood movies, and on Saturdays idle their time away at
"milkbars" and "hot-dog counters" smoking "secret
cigarettes" and "daring gins and lime" [p. 33]. They
often complete their boredom by visiting the Johannesburg
Zoo Lake, where they hang around and engage in hasty,
frivolous sexual encounters.

In discussing this group of whites, La Guma portrays
an inferior people who are benefiting from a system that
has unjustly dispossessed the majority. Furthermore,
although the English settlers are aware of the injustice
being perpetrated against the majority, they simply wrap
themselves in a cocoon and ignore the problems of the
country. The English settlers are bloodsuckers or
"ticks" twice over: first they live off the backs of an
Afrikaner-devised system of apartheid that ensures rights
and privileges to all whites, and second, like the Afrikaners they live off the backs of stolen black land and
cheap black labor. Yet they disassociate themselves from
the formulation of the system of apartheid and accuse the
Afrikaners of the cruelty and injustice perpetrated
against blacks, and they treat the blacks with contempt
but argue always that they are not racists in the manner
that the Afrikaners are. In bringing about the death of
Stopes in the manner in which it occurs in the novel, La
Guma contends "that the attitude of the English settler
to the blacks is not dissimilar to the Afrikaners and
Stopes' death is as inevitable as Meulen's if South
Africa is to be cleansed of negative forces" (8).

As in And a Threefold Cord, La Guma again displays
his uncanny ability to use nature as an important
presence that comments on the general theme and parallels
the attitude of the people in Time of the Butcherbird.
In the earlier book, the cold winter rain of the Cape has
an overwhelming presence and the good or bad fortunes of
the poorly clad, badly housed slum dwellers are dependent
on whether the rain falls or lets up. In Time of the
Butcherbird, there is no rain but a catastrophic
drought, which symbolizes as well the barren arena where
the conflicting communities act out their cruelty and
their resistance. Just like the two roads that bisect
each other "like scars of a branded cross on the pocked

and powdered skin of the earth," the two contending communities have assembled on the "flat and featureless"
plain of the drought-stricken Karoo to act out an important phase of South African history [p. 1]. In And a
Threefold Cord, when the rain finally stops a new baby
is born, signifying hope and man's ability to weather
the rainstorm. In Time of the Butcherbird, when the
drought nears its end and a hint of rain is indicated,
hope is suggested by the fact that the oppressed blacks
have heeded Mma-Tau's call to resist enslavement and to
become militant again as in the days of the ancestors.
Hence the drought of resigned and humiliating defeat at
the hands of the oppressors is finally transformed into
hopeful rain.

Time of the Butcherbird depicts the drought in vivid
and despairing portraits. Although "a country of flat,
weary distances scattered with stunted karoo bush that
crumbled underfoot like rotten wood and left small
hollows of red earth," it has defied "the remorseless
sun" and has bred "kudu and leopard" and given a home
to the "green or brown mamba," the "red spiders," the
"scrub and whitethorn," and the sheep [p. 14]. But now
even this defiance, like that of Hlangeni's people,
seems to be wilting away as the drought takes its toll
[p. 16]. The sheep, without grazing land, are close to
death, and the dog guarding them is a shadow of its
former self [pp. 16-17].

The general despair that embraces this natural setting
is compared to the human despair that has been brought
about by inhuman behavior on the part of the Afrikaner
government, its followers, and the mining investors. The
remnants of Hlangeni's people, whose ancestors once
defied the sun-drenched land and thrived on the barren
land, are now reduced to landless people accepting in
resignation their dispossessed state and, like the
mongrel dog, shy away from challenging the unjust state
and instead break out in feeble song. Such a people
stand to be insulted by the puny clerk of the commissioner, by the commissioner himself, and by the uncouth
young boy on a cycle who sprays Kobe and his companion
with red dust.

The dominee contends that the drought is caused by the
Afrikaners' failure to uphold God's laws of racial purity
and moral living and declares a day of prayer for rain.
At the end of a self-righteous, hypocritical service, the
Afrikaner men continue the human drought by carting away

Hlangeni and his remnants to a dusty, "flat and feature-less" land. Mma-Tau observes the hypocrisy of this prayer for rain by referring to the human drought that exists in the hearts of Afrikaners. And speaking out of the belief that heartless men cannot understand the hurt and wrong they inflict on others, she calls upon the people to stop waiting on government decrees, Afrikaner goodwill, and even prayer to end the human drought. She sends out a call for forceful resistance and just strug-gle to return again to the blacks the land that belongs to them. And as the resistance movement spreads to the Karoo hills and to the urban centers, it "seems that the air, heavy with heat, begins to move." Nature is sympa-thetic to those who use her resources properly. The Karoo will turn to fertility again once the greed of the Afrikaners has been quelled. And prayer services will only be of use when one community does not use another to further its aims. When the drought in man's heart is replaced by genuine concern for every person regardless of color, then the "flight of birds [will] swoop overhead towards a water-hole" [p. 119].

As in the previous books, La Guma does not leave the reader with a completely negative view of a country that has been trading in negative aspects of human nature for hundreds of years. The dismal, dreary world of the resigned dispossessed of the first scene of the novel is counteracted at the end by the defiance of those who heed Mma-Tau's call to resist enslavement and dispossession. And like the song of the butcherbird the songs are now of hope and defiance as opposed to the songs of resignation in the opening scene. The cruel, natural drought that dominates most of the scenery of the book seems to be dissipating at the end, thus signifying fertility and hope. The hateful personal revenge of Shilling Murile is transformed into collective purpose and struggle. For the time being the "bisecting roads" of white and black aspirations are still "branded cross[es]," but once the butcherbird has cleansed the entire society of its nega-tive aspects, a time of joy will finally come.

Chapter Eight
Conclusion

Since 1957 Alex La Guma has produced fourteen short stories, five novels, and a travel book on the Soviet Union. In addition, he has written numerous essays on the political struggle in South Africa and edited a collection of writings on apartheid. His work has been translated into fifteen languages, demonstrating the value of his creative contributions. As a creative artist who addresses the central questions of life in South Africa, he has established himself as an important literary figure both in Africa and in the rest of the world.

His political life, which has always taken precedence over his creative career, has kept pace with his artistic one. He has, since 1947, been in the forefront of militant opposition to the racist policies of the South African regime. He has been an executive member of the antiracist congress movement since 1954 and is currently the representative of the Liberation Movement in the Caribbean. His deep-felt belief that the system of apartheid is unjust to the majority of South Africans has led to his being tried for treason, imprisoned on several occasions, and detained in near-solitary confinement in his own home. But no amount of punishment by the racist regime has succeeded in destroying his vision of a South Africa free of discrimination and oppression. His task has always been that of supporting the forces that will bring about the liberation of men, women, and children in South Africa on social, economic, political, and cultural levels. To this end, he has created in his books memorable characters and situations that portray South Africa in all its human ugliness, defiance, and hope.

It is fitting that La Guma should at present continue to combine his political work in Cuba with his creation of a new novel. It is logical as well that he should continue to pursue the theme of resistance, which preoccupied him in In the Fog of the Season's End and Time of the Butcherbird. Since the student and then mass uprisings in South Africa in 1976, the country has become a

136

place where the oppressed have become more militant and
where they have taken their battles to the street. In
the novel, tentatively known as "Zone of Fire," La Guma
envisions a country where the trained cadres of the Liberation Movement have returned to South Africa to do deci-
sive battle against the oppressor community. With the
assistance of the now aware and defiant oppressed of
Time of the Butcherbird, the revolutionary struggle is
about to enter its last phase and end in triumph. At the
end of the road will be the birth of a new, nonracial
South Africa where all South Africans can live in
harmony. This is what La Guma has longed for all his
life; and, one hopes, this is what he will live to see in
his own day.

Notes and References

Preface

1. "Culture and Liberation," World Literature Written in English 18, no. 1 (April 1979):27.

Chapter One

1. Unpublished Interview, Havana, June 1981. On March 24, 1978, and from June 1-10, 1981, I interviewed Alex La Guma extensively at his respective homes in London and Havana. I shall refer to each of these interviews as Unpublished Interview and note the place and date of its occurrence.
2. Ibid.
3. Ibid.
4. Ibid.
5. Unpublished Interview, London, March 1978.
6. Ibid.
7. Ibid.
8. Ibid.
9. Unpublished Interview, Havana, June 1981.
10. Unpublished Interview, London, March 1978.
11. Ibid.
12. Ibid.
13. Ibid.
14. Ibid.
15. Ibid.
16. Ibid.
17. In the Fog of the Season's End (London: Heinemann, 1972), p. 40. Henceforth all quotations from this work will be cited in the text.
18. Unpublished Interview, London, March 1978.
19. Ibid.
20. Ibid.
21. Unpublished Interview, Havana, June 1981.
22. Ibid.
23. Ibid.
24. Ibid.
25. Ibid.
26. Ibid.

27. Blanche La Guma, Unpublished Interview, Havana, June 1981.

28. Ibid.

29. Ibid.

30. Unpublished Interview, Havana, June 1981.

31. New Age 1, no. 37 (July 7, 1955):5.

32. Ibid.

33. Ibid., p. 7.

34. New Age 1, no. 50 (October 6, 1955):3.

35. New Age 2, no. 25 (April 19, 1956):1.

36. New Age 2, no. 26 (April 26, 1956):3.

37. Unpublished Interview, London, March 1978.

38. R. K. Cope, "Objectives," New Age 1, no. 1 (October 28, 1954):1.

39. "A Pick and Shovel," New Age 2, no. 44 (September 30, 1956):3.

40. Ibid.

41. "The Dead End Kids of Hanover Street," New Age 2, no. 47 (September 20, 1956):6.

42. "What Goes On in Roeland Street Jail," New Age 2, no. 48 (September 27, 1956):6.

43. "A Day at Court," New Age 2, no. 53 (November 1, 1956):6.

44. "Don't Sneeze—the Walls May Fall Down," New Age 2, no. 54 (November 8, 1956):5.

45. "They All Have Their Troubles, but Nobody Complains," New Age, January 24, 1957, pp. 4-5.

46. "Up My Alley," New Age, May 23, 1957, p. 7.

47. Ibid., New Age, September 26, 1957, p. 6.

48. Ibid., New Age, October 10, 1957, p. 5.

49. New Age, May 15, 1958, p. 1.

50. Ibid.

51. Unpublished Interview, London, March 1978.

52. Ibid.

53. Unpublished Interview, Havana, June 1981.

54. Ibid.

55. Ibid.

56. Unpublished Interview, London, March 1978.

57. Ibid.

58. Ibid.

59. Ibid.

60. Unpublished Interview, Havana, June 1981.

61. Ibid.

62. Ibid.

63. Ibid.

64. Ibid.

Chapter Two

1. Unpublished Interview, London, March 1978.
2. Unpublished Interview, Havana, June 1981.
3. Bernth Lindfors, "Form and Technique in the Novels of Richard Rive and Alex La Guma," New African Literature and the Arts, ed. J. Okpaku (New York, 1966), p. 44. Throughout the book I shall show that La Guma believes that the South African society with its oppressive race division is chiefly instrumental in the downfall of the individuals of the society. Unlike Lindfors, however, I agree with La Guma that he does not "set out to create heroes among the oppressed."
4. Unpublished Interview, Havana, June 1981.
5. "Out of Darkness," in Quartet, ed. R. Rive (London, 1965), p. 33. Henceforth all quotations from this work will be cited in the text.
6. Unpublished Interview, Havana, June 1981.
7. "Nocturne," in Quartet, p. 112. Subsequent quotations are cited in the text.
8. "A Glass of Wine," in Quartet, p. 91. Subsequent quotations are cited in the text.
9. Unpublished Interview, Havana, June 1981.
10. Ibid.
11. "Slipper Satin," in Quartet, p. 68. Subsequent quotations are cited in the text.
12. "The Gladiators," in A Walk in the Night and Other Stories (London, 1968), p. 114. Subsequent quotations are cited in the text.
13. Unpublished Interview, Havana, June 1981.
14. "The Lemon Orchard," in A Walk in the Night and Other Stories, p. 134. Subsequent quotations are cited in the text.
15. Unpublished Interview, Havana, June 1981.
16. Ibid.
17. "Coffee for the Road," in Modern African Stories, ed. E. A. Komey and E. Mphahele (London, 1964), p. 87. Subsequent quotations are cited in the text.
18. "At the Portagee's," in A Walk in the Night and Other Stories, pp. 108-9. Subsequent quotations are cited in the text.
19. "A Matter of Taste," in A Walk in the Night and Other Stories, pp. 126-27. Subsequent quotations are cited in the text.
20. Unpublished Interview, Havana, June 1981.
21. Ibid.

22. "A Matter of Honour," New Nation 4, no. 7 (September 1965):170.

23. "Tattoo Marks and Nails," in A Walk in the Night and Other Stories, p. 100. Subsequent quotations are cited in the text.

24. "Blankets," in A Walk in the Night and Other Stories, p. 121.

25. "Thang's Bicycle," Lotus: Afro-Asian Writings 29 (July-September 1976):42-47.

Chapter Three

1. Unpublished Interview, Havana, June 1981.

2. Several critics have commented on the form and technique of A Walk in the Night. J. Okpure Obuke, in "The Structure of Commitment: A Study of Alex La Guma," Ba Shiru 5, no. 1 (1973):14, contends that "Alex La Guma is essentially a short story writer who depends for his effect in rapidly building up short, graphic and dramatic scenes. In A Walk in the Night, La Guma attempts to manipulate the same short story narrative technique to fit much more complex and wider canvas than that of the short story." Lewis Nkosi, in "Fiction by Black South Africans," in Home and Exile (London: Longmans, 1965), p. 125, sees "distinct Dostoevskian undertones" in the novel. Michael Wade, in "Art and Morality in Alex La Guma's A Walk in the Night," in The South African Novel in English, ed. K. Parker (London: Macmillan, 1979), pp. 165-66, sees in La Guma's "writing a concern for artistic method and technique every bit as obsessional as, say, that which characterizes the early fiction of Nadine Gordimer." And Robert Green, in "Chopin in the Ghetto: The Short Stories of Alex La Guma," WLWE 20, no. 1 (1981):12, complains about A Walk in the Night's failure to "satisfy either of the reader's two expectations—for brevity and the episodic, or for amplitude and coherence." Green goes on to say (p. 14): "The fortuitous, the random and the contingent lie at the heart of the novella's content and these same qualities define the tale's form, its circularity and jerkiness." As I observe in the chapter on And a Three-fold Cord, La Guma does not make a distinction between writing a short story and a long one: "I never really consciously thought of producing a novel, as such, in terms of the formal structures and so on. . . . I just

constructed the whole story in my mind, whether it was a
short story or a long story." La Guma also notes that at
the time of writing A Walk in the Night he was a
journalist and that "it was inevitable that the style of
the journalist would crop up." Furthermore, since "it
was my first attempt at a lengthy work, perhaps it's what
one calls a sort of popular writing in the popular press
for a general audience."

3. Unpublished Interview, London, March 1978.

4. "The Dead-End Kids of Hanover Street," New Age
2, no. 47 (September 20, 1956):6.

5. Unpublished Interview, London, March 1978.

6. Ibid.

7. Unpublished Interview, Havana, June 1981.

8. "Dedication," in A Walk in the Night and Other
Stories. The "realistic nature" of the novel has been
commented upon by several critics. Bernth Lindfors, in
"Robin Hood Realism in South African English Fiction,"
Africa Today 15, no. 4 (1968):18, observes that "most
of [La Guma's] heroes are men made criminals by their
environment." Chris Wanjala, in "The Face of Injustice:
Alex La Guma's Fiction," in Standpoints on African Literature (Nairobi: East African Literature Bureau, 1973),
p. 310, says that "in every face of every character in A
Walk in the Night the reader sees marks of woe owing to
the oppressive apartheid system." David Rabkin in "La
Guma and Reality in South Africa," Journal of Commonwealth Literature 8, no. 1 (1973):55, is only partially
correct when he says that "La Guma's purpose is to
enlarge our understanding, not of the characters, but of
their situation." And J. Okpure, in "The Structure of
Commitment: A Study of Alex La Guma," Ba Shiru 5, no.
1 (1973):15, puts it best when he says: "La Guma's
primary concern is with the present predicament of the
inhabitants of District Six. In A Walk in the Night,
he attempts to show what has happened to the people who
live in the oppressive system of apartheid."

9. Unpublished Interview, Havana, June 1981.

10. Unpublished Interview, London, March 1978.

11. A Walk in the Night, p. 1. Subsequent quotations are cited in the text.

12. Unpublished Interview, Havana, June 1981.

13. Ibid.

14. Unpublished Interview, London, March 1978.

15. Unpublished Interview, Havana, June 1981.

Chapter Four

1. Unpublished Interview, Havana, June 1981.

2. Unpublished Interview, London, March 1978. Gerald Moore, in Twelve African Writers (Bloomington: Indiana University Press, 1980), p. 110, sees a difference in the creation of the short story and the novel and says that "the increased scope of the novel brings from the author a greater degree of commitment."

3. Ibid.

4. Ibid.

5. Unpublished Interview, Havana, June 1981.

6. Ibid.

7. Ibid.

8. Ibid.

9. B. Bunting, Foreword, And a Threefold Cord (Berlin, 1964), p. 15.

10. Unpublished Interview, Havana, June 1981.

11. Ibid.

12. Although Charlie Pauls is the chief single character through whom La Guma records his message of challenge, he is not "a hero" as suggested by Gerald Moore in Twelve African Writers, p. 111.

13. And a Threefold Cord, p. 18. Subsequent quotations are cited in the text.

14. Unpublished Interview, Havana, June 1981.

15. Ibid.

16. Ibid.

Chapter Five

1. Unpublished Interview, London, March 1978.

2. Dedication, The Stone Country (London, 1974). Subsequent quotations are cited in the text.

3. Unpublished Interview, London, March 1978.

4. Unpublished Interview, Havana, June 1981.

5. Ibid.

6. Ibid.

7. "Tattoo Marks and Nails," in A Walk in the Night and Other Stories, pp. 97-107; "Out of Darkness," in Quartet, pp. 34-35.

8. Unpublished Interview, Havana, June 1981.

9. Ibid. Dieter Riemenschneider, in his essay "The Prisoner in South African Fiction: Alex La Guma's The Stone Country and In the Fog of the Season's End," in Individual and Community in Commonwealth Literature,

ed. Daniel Massa (Msida, 1979), pp. 51-58, rightfully sees Adams's role as that of a catalyst.

Chapter Six

1. Unpublished Interview, Havana, June 1981.
2. In the Fog of the Season's End (London, 1972), pp. 180-81. Subsequent quotations are cited in the text.
3. Unpublished Interview, London, March 1978.
4. Cited in frontispiece to In the Fog of the Season's End.
5. Critics seem to differ in regard to this point. Leonard Kibera in "A Critical Appreciation of Alex La Guma's In the Fog of the Season's End," Busara 8, no. 1 (1976):66, sees the work as "a major achievement in African literature" because "of the complexities of revolutionary commitment." David Rabkin in "La Guma and Reality in South Africa," Journal of Commonwealth Literature 8, no. 1 (1973):60-61, sees this novel as being less successful because it is more blatantly concerned with ideology rather than art; whereas Gerald Moore in Twelve African Writers, p. 118, considers this to be La Guma's most mature, "finest," and "moving" novel.
6. Unpublished Interview, London, March 1978.
7. Ibid.
8. Unpublished Interview, Havana, June 1981.
9. Ibid.
10. Ibid.
11. La Guma and his wife, Blanche, refer hilariously to their days of courtship.
12. Unpublished Interview, Havana, June 1981.
13. Ibid.
14. Rabkin, "La Guma and Reality in African Literature," p. 61.
15. Moore, Twelve African Writers, p. 118; Kibera, "A Critical Appreciation of Alex La Guma's In the Fog of the Season's End," p. 66.

Chapter Seven

1. Unpublished Interview, Havana, June 1981.
2. Time of the Butcherbird (London, 1979), dedication. Subsequent quotations are cited in the text.
3. Unpublished Interview, Havana, June 1981.
4. Ibid.
5. Ibid. Gerald Moore in Twelve African Writers,

p. 118, says that <u>Time of the Butcherbird</u> returns in
manner to the short stories and <u>A Walk in the Night</u>.
It must be assumed that Moore means that La Guma is less
explicit and blatant in dealing with the South African
situation than in the other books. If so, I think Moore
is wrong, for although the subject is not treated as
directly as in <u>In the Fog of the Season's End</u>, it is
devastatingly powerful in its condemnation of injustice.

6. Ibid.
7. Unpublished Interview, Havana, June 1981.
8. Ibid.

Selected Bibliography

PRIMARY SOURCES
(arranged as written)

1. Short Stories
"Etude." New Age, January 24, 1957, p. 6. Later
    reprinted in Quartet as "Nocturne." Edited by R.
    Rive. London: Heinemann, 1965, pp. 111-16.
"Out of Darkness." Africa South 2, no. 1 (October
    1957):118-22. Later reprinted in Quartet, pp.
    33-38.
"A Glass of Wine." Black Orpheus 7 (1960):22-25.
    Later reprinted in Quartet, pp. 91-96.
"Slipper Satin." Black Orpheus 8 (1960):32-35. Later
    reprinted in Quartet, pp. 67-73.
"A Matter of Taste." In A Walk in the Night and Other
    Stories. London: Heinemann, 1967, pp. 125-30.
"At the Portagee's." Black Orpheus 11 (1963):18-21.
    Later reprinted in A Walk in the Night and Other
    Stories, pp. 108-13.
"Tattoo Marks and Nails." Black Orpheus 14 (1964):48-
    53. Later reprinted in A Walk in the Night and Other
    Stories, pp. 97-107.
"The Lemon Orchard." In A Walk in the Night and Other
    Stories, pp. 131-36.
"Blankets." Black Orpheus 15 (1964):57-58. Later
    reprinted in African Writing Today. Edited by E.
    Mphahlele. Harmondsworth: Penguin, 1967, pp. 268-73;
    and A Walk in the Night and Other Stories, pp. 121-
    24.
"Coffee for the Road." In Modern African Stories.
    Edited by E. A. Komey and E. Mphahlele. London:
    Faber & Faber, 1964, pp. 85-94.
"A Matter of Honour." New African 4, no. 7 (1965):167-
    70.
"The Gladiators." In A Walk in the Night and Other
    Stories, pp. 114-20.
"Late Edition." Lotus: Afro-Asian Writings 29 (1976):
    42-47.

"Thang's Bicycle." <u>Lotus: Afro-Asian Writings</u> 29
(1976):42-47.

2. Novels
<u>A Walk in the Night.</u> Ibadan: Mbari, 1962. Reprinted
simultaneously by Heinemann, London, and Northwestern
University Press, Evanston, Illinois, as <u>A Walk in
the Night and Other Stories</u>, 1967.
<u>And a Threefold Cord.</u> Berlin: Seven Seas, 1964.
<u>The Stone Country.</u> Berlin: Seven Seas, 1967. Re-
printed in Heinemann's African Writers Series, 1974.
<u>In the Fog of the Season's End.</u> London: Heinemann,
1972.
<u>Time of the Butcherbird.</u> London: Heinemann, 1979.

3. Other Books Written or Edited by Alex La Guma
<u>Apartheid.</u> Edited. London: Lawrence & Wishart, 1971.
<u>A Soviet Journey.</u> Moscow: Progress Books, 1978.

4. Articles, Interviews, Lectures
"Blind Alley." <u>Drum</u>, January 1956, pp. 33-34.
"Down the Quiet Street." <u>Drum</u>, January 1956, pp. 46-
48.
"A Pick and Shovel." <u>New Age</u> 2, no. 44 (September 30,
1956):3.
"The Dead End Kids of Hanover Street." <u>New Age</u> 2, no.
47 (September 20, 1956):6.
"What Goes On in Roeland Street Jail." <u>New Age</u> 2, no.
48 (September 27, 1956):6.
"The Machine." <u>Fighting Talk</u> 12, no. 10 (October
1956):8-9.
"A Day at Court." <u>New Age</u> 2, no. 53 (November 1,
1956):6.
"Don't Sneeze—the Walls May Fall Down." <u>New Age</u> 2,
no. 54 (November 8, 1956):5.
"A Christmas Story." <u>Fighting Talk</u> 10, no. 11 (Decem-
ber 1956-January 1957):6.
"They All Have Their Troubles, but Nobody Complains."
<u>New Age</u> 3, no. 4 (January 24, 1957):4-5.
"Battle for Honour." <u>Drum</u>, November 1958, pp. 85 ff.
"Up My Alley." <u>New Age</u>. A regular weekly column,
interrupted by attendance at treason trial and deten-
tions, from May 2, 1957, until June 28, 1962.
Interview with Robert Serumaga. <u>Cultural Events in
Africa</u> 24 (1966):i-ii supp.
"The Time Has Come." <u>Sechaba</u> 1, no. 3 (1967):14-15; 1,

no. 4 (1967):13-14; 1, no. 5 (1967):14-16; no. 6 (1967):15-16.

"The Third Afro-Asian Writers' Conference." Cultural Events in Africa 29 (1967):4-5.

"The Writer in a Modern African State." In The Writer in Modern Africa. Edited by P. Wastberg. New York: Africana Publishing, 1969, pp. 21-24.

"African Culture and Liberation." Journal of the New African Literature and the Arts 7 and 8 (1970):99-101.

"Come Back to Tashkent." Lotus: African-Asian Writings 1, no. 4 (1970):208-10.

"Literature and Life." Lotus: Afro-Asian Writings 1, no. 4 (1970):237-39.

"Address by Lotus Award Winner." Lotus: Afro-Asian Writings 10 (1971):195-97.

"The Condition of Culture in South Africa." Présence Africaine 80 (1971):113-22.

Interview with Mazisi Kunene. In African Writers Talking. Edited by D. Duerden and C. Pieterse. London: Heinemann, 1972, p. 88.

"The Exile." Lotus: Afro-Asian Writings 11 (1972):68-75.

"On Short Stories." Lotus: Afro-Asian Writings 17 (1973):132-33.

"African Culture and National Liberation." In New African Literature and the Arts, vol. 3. Edited by Joseph Okpaku. New York: The Third Press, 1973.

"In Memory of Hutch: Alfred Hutchinson (South Africa)." Lotus: Afro-Asian Writings 17 (1973):135.

"Sounds of a Cowhide Drum by Oswald Joseph Mtshali." Lotus: Afro-Asian Writings 21 (1974):180-87.

"Kultur und Apartheid in Sudafrika." IKA: Zeitschrift fur Internationalen Kulturanstausch (Stuttgart) 1 (1974):5-10.

"I Came Here to Sing: A Tribute to Pablo Neruda." Lotus: Afro-Asian Writings 22 (1974):145-47.

"South African Writing under Apartheid." Lotus: Afro-Asian Writings 23 (1975):11-21.

"Culture and Liberation." Sechaba 10, no. 4 (1976):50-58.

"Where Have All the Flowers Gone: Censorship in South Africa." Lotus: Afro-Asian Writings 25 (1976):16-23.

"For a Better and New World." Moscow News, October 22, 1978, p. 14.

"Culture and Liberation." World Literature Written in
    English 18, no. 1 (April 1979):27-36.
"An Assessment of Tolstoy." Moscow Literary Gazette,
    June 1980, pp. 7-9.
"A Portrait of Myself." Moscow Literary Gazette, Novem-
    ber 1980, pp. 4-6.

5. Unpublished Essays and Interviews
"Paul Robeson and Africa." Berlin, April 1971.
"Has Art Failed in South Africa?" London, 1973.
"What do you read in Apartheid South Africa?" London,
    1975.
Interview with Cecil Abrahams. London, March 1978.
Interview with Cecil Abrahams. Havana, June 1981.

SECONDARY SOURCES

1. Books
Beier, Ulli, ed. Introduction to African Literature.
    London: Longman, 1967. Contains essays on African
    literature in general.
Cartey, Wilfred. Whispers from a Continent. New York:
    Random House, 1969. Broad survey of African litera-
    ture and a discussion of La Guma's stories and first
    two novels.
Dathorne, O. R. African Literature in the Twentieth
    Century. London: Heinemann, 1976. Covers many
    areas of African literature, but deals superficially
    with La Guma's early work.
Duerden, Dennis, and Pieterse, Cosmo, eds. African
    Writers Talking: A Collection of Radio Interviews.
    London: Heinemann, 1972. Sixteen radio interviews
    with African writers, including La Guma.
Gakwandi, S. A. The Novel and Contemporary Experience
    in Africa. London: Heinemann, 1977. A critical
    assessment of twelve African novels, including A Walk
    in the Night.
Herdeck, D. E. African Authors: A Companion to Black
    African Writing. Vol. 1: 1300-1973. Washington,
    D.C.: Black Orpheus, 1973. Useful bibliographical
    information on many writers, including La Guma.
Heywood, Christopher, ed. Aspects of South African
    Literature. London: Heinemann, 1976. Contains a
    few good essays on South African writing.
Klima, Vladimir. South African Prose Writing in
    English. Prague: Oriental Institute, 1971. Dis-

cusses La Guma and several other South African writers' works.

Lindfors, B., ed. Black African Literature in English: A Guide to Information Sources. Detroit: Gale Research Company, 1979. A comprehensive bibliography that covers most aspects of African literature.

Moore, Gerald. Twelve African Writers. Bloomington: Indiana University Press, 1980. Contains a good chapter on La Guma's work.

Mphahlele, Es'kia. The African Image. London: Faber, 1962 and 1974. Covers many aspects of African literature, including a discussion of La Guma's work.

_____. Voices in the Whirlwind and Other Essays. New York: Hill & Wang, 1972. Essays on African literature and censorship in South Africa.

Nkosi, Lewis. Home and Exile. London and Ibadan: Longman, 1965. Essays on South Africa and life in exile.

_____. The Transplanted Heart: Essays on South Africa. Benin City: Ethiope Publishing, 1975. Contains a short but perceptive essay on La Guma's work.

Parker, Kenneth, ed. The South African Novel in English: Essays in Criticism and Society. New York: Africana Publishing Company, 1978. Contains a wrong-headed essay on A Walk in the Night.

Pieterse, Cosmo, and Munro, Donald, eds. Protest and Conflict in African Literature. London: Heinemann, 1969. Contains several essays that demonstrate the importance of protest in African literature.

Roscoe, A. A. Uhuru's Fire: African Literature East to South. Cambridge: Cambridge University Press, 1977. Contains a few elementary remarks on La Guma and discusses two of his novels.

Soyinka, Wole. Myth, Literature and the African World. Cambridge: Cambridge University Press, 1976. A wide-ranging book on African myth, literature, and the African world. The book discusses A Walk in the Night as social reality.

Wanjala, C. L., ed. Standpoints on African Literature. Nairobi: East African Literature Bureau, 1973. Contains a good essay on La Guma's work.

Wästberg, Per, ed. The Writer in Modern Africa: African-Scandinavian Writers' Conference, Stockholm 1967. Uppsala: Scandinavian Institute of African Studies, 1968. Papers from a conference on African writing. La Guma speaks on the connection between his writing and the political reality in South Africa.

Zell, H. M., and Silver, H., eds. A Reader's Guide to
African Literature. London: Heinemann, 1972. Anno-
tated bibliography of books, including biography of La
Guma.

2. Essays and Reviews

Abrahams, Cecil A. "Achebe, Ngugi and La Guma: Commitment and the Traditional Storyteller." Mana Review
2, no. 1 (1977):11-24. Shows the influence of the
oral tradition on the writers.

_____. "The Literature of Victims in South Africa."
Literary Criterion 13, no. 2 (1978):59-72. Contains
a discussion of In the Fog of the Season's End.

_____. "Literature and Commitment: African Perspec-
tives." In Individual and Community. Edited by D.
Massa. Msida: University Press, 1979, pp. 59-68.
The essay discusses commitment in African literature
and looks at La Guma's work.

_____. "The Context of Black South African Litera-
ture." World Literature Written in English 18, no.
1 (April 1979):18-19. Shows the mainsprings of black
South African writing and uses among others La Guma's
work.

_____. "The Literature of Apartheid." In Linguis-
tique, Civilization, Littérature. Edited by L.
Leclaire. Paris: Didier, 1980. The essay deals with
the effects of apartheid on South African writers,
including La Guma.

_____. "Literature and Politics: The South African
Example." CARIB, no. 2 (1981):1-8. Demonstrates
the importance of politics in South African literature.

_____. "Western Literary Criticism and African
Creative Writing." In African Literature in English:
Development and Identity. Edited by A. L. McLeod,
pp. 10-22. Lawrenceville, N.J.: Rider College Press,
1981. The essay discusses perceptions of critics
trained in Western literary criticism and uses among
others La Guma's work.

_____. "South African Society as Major Character in
Alex La Guma's And a Threefold Cord." A paper
presented to the African Literature Association conference, Washington, D.C., April 1982. Discusses the
importance of the sociopolitical environment in La
Guma's novel.

_____. "Alex La Guma's Revolutionary Novels." A paper presented to the conference of the Association of Caribbean Studies, Havana, July 1982. Discusses the growth of revolution in La Guma's work.

_____. "Schweitzerism: The African Writer and the Western Critic." In Literature and Language in Multi-cultural Contexts. Edited by S. Nandan, pp. 1-10. Suva: University of the South Pacific Press, 1983. Shows how poorly Western critics have interpreted African writing.

Asein, S. O. "The Revolutionary Vision in Alex La Guma's Novels." Lotus: Afro-Asian Writings 24 & 25 (1975):9-21. Argues that in La Guma's case literature cannot be divorced from the South African reality.

Astrachan, A. M. "Review of A Walk in the Night." Black Orpheus 14 (1964):59. A slight review that summarizes the novel.

Banham, M. "Review of A Walk in the Night." Books Abroad 36, no. 4 (1962):458. A slight review of the novel.

Bunting, B. Foreword to And a Threefold Cord, pp. 9-16. Berlin: Seven Seas Books, 1964. Talks about the writer and the political environment in South Africa.

Calder, A. "Living Objects: A Review of In the Fog of the Season's End." New Statesman, November 3, 1972. A superficial view of the novel.

Cartey, W. "Review of And a Threefold Cord." African Forum 1, no. 3 (1966):115-21. Apart from a slight reference to plot, the review is not of much value.

Chennels, A. "Alex La Guma and the South African Political Novel." Mambo Review of Contemporary African Literature 1 (1973):14-16. Places the writer and his work in the context of South African politics.

Coetzee, J. M. "Alex La Guma and the responsibilities of the South African Writer." Journal of the New African Literature and the Arts 9 & 10 (1971):5-11. The essay shows how La Guma confronts the issues in South African life.

_____. "Man's Fate in the Novels of Alex La Guma." Studies in Black Literature 5, no. 1 (1974):16-23. A good essay that looks at characters in La Guma's work.

Couzens, T. "Literature by Black South Africans: Our Crippling Codes." New Nation 4, no. 6 (1971):9-13.

This survey covers writers such as La Guma, Dhlomo, and Plaatje.

Dett, V. S. "New South African Literature—1967: A Critical Chronicle." English Studies in Africa 11, no. 1 (1968):61-69. Surveys the work of new South African writers in 1967, including La Guma's.

Egudu, R. N. "African Literature and Social Problems." Canadian Journal of African Studies 9, no. 3 (1975): 421-47. Shows how in a time of turbulence mingled with sharp rebellion and the nostalgic yearning for freedom superb artistic works have been created.

El-Sebai, Y. "The Role of Afro-Asian Literature and the National Liberation Movements." Afro-Asian Writings 1, no. 1 (1968):5-12. Shows how the liberation movements relate to the protest literature of the day.

_____. "The Lotus Prize: A Distinctive Landmark of Our Movement." Lotus: Afro-Asian Writings 12 (1972):8-9. Discusses the work of La Guma and others who have won the Lotus prize for literature.

Fatton, K. "The Song in the Barren Land: A Study of the Metaphors in Time of the Butcherbird." A paper presented to the African Literature Association conference, Claremont College, Claremont, California, April 1981, pp. 1-15. A good study of the metaphors in the novel.

Fourie, S. "Across the Colour Line: Some Remarks on South African Writing." African Communist 19 (1964):77-85. Argues that the revolt against apartheid has affected literature as well. Surveys some black writers, including La Guma.

Gérard, A. "Towards a History of South African Literature." In Commonwealth Literature and the Modern World. Edited by Hena Maes-Jelinek. Brussels: Didier, 1975, pp. 79-88. A few elementary comments about black writers in South Africa.

Gordimer, N. "Themes and Attitudes in Modern African Writing." Michigan Quarterly Review 9 (1970):221-29. Discusses several African writers, including La Guma.

_____. "English-Language Literature and Politics in South Africa." In Aspects of South African Literature. Edited by C. Heywood. London: Heinemann, 1976, pp. 99-120. A good essay dealing with politics and literature.

Green, R. J. "Alex La Guma's In the Fog of the Season's End: The Politics of Subversion." Umoja 3, no. 2

(1979):85-93. Makes the connection between literature and politics.

_____. "Chopin in the Ghetto: The Short Stories of Alex La Guma." World Literature Written in English 20, no. 1 (1981):5-17. A superficial, misleading article.

Hetherington, J. "The Concept of the Individual as Hero in Modern African Literature." AFRAS 1, no. 3 (1972):18-22. Deals with the idealization of characters in black South African writing.

Izevbaye, A. S. "African Literature Defined: The Record of a Controversy." Ibadan Studies in English 1 (1969):56-69. Discussion of assumptions underlying definitions of African literature.

Jan Mohammed, Abdul R. "Alex La Guma: The Generation of Marginal Fiction." In Manichean Aesthetics, pp. 225-62. Amherst: The University of Massachusetts Press, 1983. Discusses La Guma's political and creative lives.

July, R. W. "The African Personality in the African Novel." In Introduction to African Literature. Edited by U. Beier. London: Longman, 1967, pp. 218-21. A discussion of A Walk in the Night.

Kibera, L. "A Critical Appreciation of Alex La Guma's In the Fog of the Season's End." Busara 8, no. 1 (1976):59-66. A very good essay that deals effectively with the novel's purpose.

Klíma, V. "The South African Writer's Political Commitment." Archiv Orientální 42 (1974):193-99. Deals with the work of Dennis Brutus, La Guma, and Lewis Nkosi.

Lindfors, B. "Form and Technique in the Novels of Richard Rive and Alex La Guma." In New African Literature and the Arts, vol. 1. Edited by Joseph Okpaku, pp. 42-51. New York: Thomas Y. Crowell, 1966. A good essay that discusses the form and technique of the two writers.

_____. "Review of And a Threefold Cord." Books Abroad 40, no. 1 (1966):116. A short review of the novel.

_____. "Robin Hood Realism in South African English Fiction." Africa Today 15, no. 4 (1968):16-19. Discusses the work of Alex La Guma and Richard Rive.

_____. "Entry on La Guma." In Contemporary Novelists, pp. 735-36. London: St. James Press, 1972. A short biographical entry.

Maimane, Arthur. "Can't You Write about Anything Else?"
Presence Africaine 80 (1971):123-26. Writes about
the problems that black South African writers face in
creating imaginative literature in a sterile political
environment.

Mazrui, A. A. "Identity and the Novelist: An Iron Law
of Individualism." In Aspects of Africa's Identity:
Five Essays. Edited by Paul Nurse-Bray, pp. 70-79.
Kampala: Makerere University, 1973. Discusses the
work of Achebe, La Guma, Ogot, Soyinka, and others.

Mphahlele, E. "African Literature and Propaganda."
Jewel of Africa: A Literary and Cultural Magazine
from Zambia 1, nos. 4 & 5 (1968):19-23. Shows how
literature is a necessary form of propaganda.

_____. "Writers and Commitment." Black Orpheus 2,
no. 3 (1969):34-39. Discusses the commitment of
writers, including La Guma.

_____. "Tribute to Alex La Guma." Sechaba 5, no. 2
(1970):9. Praises La Guma on the occasion of winning
the Lotus prize.

Nkosi, L. "Review of And a Threefold Cord." New
African 4, no. 3 (1965):70-71. Praises La Guma's
imaginative skills.

_____. "Fiction by Black South Africans: Richard
Rive, Bloke Modisane, Ezekiel Mphahlele, Alex La
Guma." In Introduction to African Literature: An
Anthology of Critical Writing from Black Orpheus.
Edited by Ulli Beier, pp. 216-17. London: Longmans,
1967. The article discusses briefly the work of the
writers mentioned.

Obuke, J. O. "The Structure of Commitment: A Study of
Alex La Guma." Ba Shiru 5, no. 1 (1973):14-20. A
good essay on the structure of La Guma's work.

Povey, J. F. "The Political Theme in South and West
African Novels." African Quarterly 9 (1969):33-39.
Discusses literature and politics in South and West
African writings by using the work of La Guma,
Abrahams, Achebe, Aluko, and others.

_____. "Political Protest in the African Novel in
English." In Protest and Power in Black Africa.
Edited by R. I. Rothberg and A. A. Mazrui, pp. 823-53.
Discusses several African writers, including La Guma.

Rabkin, D. "La Guma and Reality in South Africa."
Journal of Commonwealth Literature 7, no. 1 (1973):
54-62. Argues rather obtusely that La Guma's work suffers because of political concerns.

Riemenschneider, D. "The Prisoner in South African Fiction: Alex La Guma's The Stone Country and In the Fog of the Season's End." In Individual and Community in Commonwealth Literature. Edited by D. Massa, pp. 51-58. Msida: University Press, 1979. A useful essay that studies the prisoner as character in La Guma's work.

Scanlon, P. A. "Alex La Guma's Novels of Protest: The Growth of the Revolutionary." OKIKE 16 (1979):39-47. Discusses La Guma as a political activist and creative artist.

Sharif, M. "The Lotus Prize Winners for the Years 1969/1970." Lotus: Afro-Asian Writings 9 (1971):94-109. Discusses the work of the Lotus prize winners, including La Guma.

Singh, R. "Sword or Pen?" Afro-Asian Writings 1, no. 4 (1970):240-41. Shows how important writing is in the struggle for liberation.

South African Exile Literature. Sechaba 5, no. 9 (1971):21-23. Comments briefly on some South African writers living in exile.

Southern African Literature and the National Struggle against Imperialist Aggression and Racial Domination. Lotus: Afro-Asian Writings 20 (1974):13-18. A statement by a South African delegation, including La Guma, emphasizing the importance of literature in the national struggle for liberation.

Visser, N. W. "South Africa: The Renaissance That Failed." Journal of Commonwealth Literature 2, no. 1 (1976):43-57. Claims but fails to show why the renaissance in literature failed.

Wade, M. "Art and Morality in Alex La Guma's A Walk in the Night." In The South African Novel in English. Edited by K. Parker, pp. 164-91. New York: Africana Publishing, 1978. A misleading and wrongheaded reading of the novel.

Wanjala, C. L. "A Literary Supplement." Joliso: East African Journal of Literature and Society 1, no. 2 (1973):1-11. Discusses socialist and capitalist aesthetics in African literature with emphasis on the work of La Guma, Ngugi, Ogot, and others.

Index